Poverty bites

Food, health and
poor families

Elizabeth Dowler and Sheila Turner
with Barbara Dobson

CPAG • 94 White Lion Street • London N1 9PF

Poverty
bites

Food, health and poor families

Elizabeth Dowler and Sheila Turner
with Barbara Dobson

CPAG • 94 White Lion Street • London N1 9PF

CPAG promotes action for the relief, directly or indirectly, of poverty among children and families with children. We work to ensure that those on low incomes get their full entitlements to welfare benefits. In our campaigning and information work we seek to improve benefits and policies for low-income families in order to eradicate the injustice of poverty. If you are not already supporting us, please consider making a donation, or ask for details of our membership schemes and publications.

Poverty Publication 105

Published by CPAG
94 White Lion Street, London N1 9PF

© CPAG 2001

ISBN 1 901698 45 9

Cover and design by Devious Designs 0114 275 5634
Typeset by Boldface 020 7253 2014
Printed by Russell Press 0115 978 4505
Cover photo by Jacky Devious Daguerreotypes

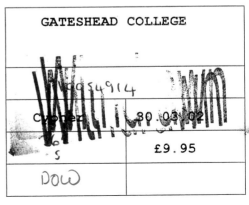

For Tony and Mike
and to the memory of Sheila Turner

ACKNOWLEDGEMENTS

Writing this book has been a challenge and a privilege. A challenge because the facts and figures are hard to pin down and present conclusively, and a privilege because they deal with the fundamentals of people's lives: what we eat and how we share it defines who we are. For many who are poor, the struggle to put something decent on the table every day is so engrained, so familiar, they cannot begin to imagine how life could be different. We have tried to capture some of that experience in this text, through people's own words as well as statistics from researchers and policy makers. We are very grateful to all those who have taken part in research projects.

We thank Child Poverty Action Group for being so patient with the gestation of this book, and for publishing the outcome, and especially Susan Brighouse, Nicola Johnston and Alison Key for seeing it through and to Paula McDiarmid for proofreading. We thank those who commented on the text: Martin Barnes, Tim Marsh, Sarah Schenker and Anna Webb, and Tim Lang for writing the foreword. We also thank the British Medical Journal, William Allen of Global Action Plan, Michelle Gocman of Enfield and Haringey Health Authority, Bill Grey of the Scottish Community Diet Project, Chris Grundy of the London School of Hygiene & Tropical Medicine, Joe Harvey of the Health Education Trust, Nina Oldfield of the Family Budget Unit and David Rex of Sandwell Health Authority, for permission to reproduce some of their material or ideas. None of those mentioned has responsibility for the text, which remains that of the authors.

Elizabeth Dowler
Sheila Turner
Barbara Dobson

SHEILA TURNER
(dec: 4 November 2000)

I asked Sheila Turner, a fellow nutritionist, to work with me on the book when my previous collaborator, Suzi Leather, had to withdraw because of other work. Sheila, who has long trained teachers and carried out research on children's views of food, was enthusiastic about the project and deeply committed to it. A diagnosis of serious illness in 1999 meant she had to do what work she could from home, which she continued to do up to her death in November 2000. It was a tremendous privilege to be discussing ideas and writing with her, during that period. She remained a stalwart and cheerful friend and colleague to the end, and taught me a great deal about the wisdom and courage of children. I miss her more than I can convey.

Barbara Dobson, of the Centre for Social Policy Research at Loughborough, had agreed to read the text when it was completed. Following Sheila's death, she helped me with the final editing and writing, during my busy first academic year at the University of Warwick. I am very grateful for her support at such a critical time.

Elizabeth Dowler

ABOUT THE AUTHORS

Elizabeth Dowler is a registered public health nutritionist, who works on the social and policy aspects of nutrition. She worked in the international arena for many years, based at the London School of Hygiene & Tropical Medicine, and brought those perspectives to bear on the UK situation over the last decade. She recently moved to the University of Warwick, where she is a senior lecturer, to address food and nutrition issues from within social policy.

Sheila Turner, who died in November 2000, was a nutritionist and Reader in Education. She was an Ofsted Inspector, teacher educator and had long experience working with children on science and technology. Her particular expertise in recent years was enabling children's voices to be heard, especially in relation to food in schools.

Barbara Dobson is Research Fellow in social policy at the Centre for Research in Social Policy, Loughborough University. She has carried out research on poverty and the experience of living on a low income, particularly the effects on food and family life, and has carried out evaluations of intervention at local and national levels.

CONTENTS

Foreword   viii

1 WHAT IS FOOD POVERTY?   1

2 CAUSES OF FOOD POVERTY   14

3 HOW DOES FOOD POVERTY AFFECT   39
   FAMILIES AND CHILDREN?

4 MANAGING TO EAT ON A LOW INCOME   67

5 WHAT IS HAPPENING TO ADDRESS   75
   FOOD POVERTY?

6 NEXT STEPS: THE CHALLENGES FOR ACTION   102

FOREWORD

That a rich country like Britain has the level of food poverty that Liz Dowler, Sheila Turner and Barbara Dobson outline in this excellent but sobering book is frankly a disgrace. My mother assured me when I was in my 20s that I would grow out of being angry about such things. Three decades later, I am surely a case of arrested development, for my anger at Britain accepting levels of food poverty which are unacceptable not only continues but grows. I dare you not to be angry at the evidence before you, too. Britain has the worst levels of food insecurity in Europe. We have the highest rates of diet-related ill-health, particularly heavy among low income groups. And yet our farming is in crisis and farm incomes are at their lowest for years. Where is the market efficiency?

For me, at a moral and emotional level, not just at an intellectual or political one, the degree of food poverty in a country is the single most important indicator of whether its food system is working. There are others of equal policy importance, of course, such as its sustainability, its financial viability, its vibrancy of food culture, the safety of its supply, the general health profile of its population, the diversity of its cuisines, and so on. But if a country cannot ensure that all its citizens are well fed, then it cannot claim to be just and it must be challenged if it dares to speak on behalf of civilisation.

In Britain, we like to think that food poverty is something that happens in far off places. As people with strong international experience and interests in nutrition, education and social policy, Drs Dowler, Turner and Dobson need no reminding about global food insecurity. They and many others, myself included, were indignant when at the time of the 1992 International Conference on Nutrition and then the 1996 World Food Summit, the British Government treated with disdain the United Nation's request for all Member States to audit their food insecurity. Britain has no food insecurity was the message that went to the world. This was and is misleading. And one of the many reasons this book is to be treasured is that it is a belated but honourable righting of the record. The truth, as this book testifies, is that there has been an heroic upsurge of community projects against and to alleviate food poverty in Britain. But fast as they build people's confidence, create solidarities, the structural problems that created the situation manufacture more victims. No one willingly experiences food poverty.

Poverty Bites, in my view, is the best summary of current understanding and data about food poverty that I know. When I read it,

I relaxed. 'That is it', I kept saying to myself. They are telling it as it is and as it needs to be told. The indignity, the ill-health, the sheer hard slog of feeding oneself and a family on low incomes. The health costs. The double burden of being surrounded by the same visual and televisual food marketing pressures as everyone else, yet not being able to purchase like them – even when it would be bad for health to do so. This is a surreal new twist to being food poor that only an 'advanced' industrial country like Britain could invent. It is normal to eat a diet that is deleterious for health in Britain. That is why the issue of food poverty has to be linked with other bids for the policy agenda – quality, prices, corporate control. As I write a Policy Commission on the Future of Food and Farming is sitting. It is to report by Christmas 2001. If food poverty, a symbol of the links between social policy and public health, is not a central part of its recommendations, an opportunity will have been lost and pressure must be put on the Government in its response to the Policy Commission to right the wrong.

The food poverty story told in these pages is both new and very old. The myths and bad faith about food poverty are legion. 'There's no food poverty in the UK, just bad management' goes one cry. Nonsense. People on low incomes are remarkable for their efficiency of purchasing and brilliance at juggling impossible demands. 'They are just badly educated and cannot cook properly'. Again, not true. My own colleagues' work shows that it is the rich, not the poor, who cook least; they can afford to buy their way out.[1]

While we read and ingest this excellent summary of a dire situation, we need to refine our thoughts. What are the policies that allow this to happen? What could be done to correct them? Which are the social forces that rely on, and defend, the indefensible? Here, as the authors show, the food poverty watchers and pressure groups have been making inroads. The poverty and health agenda has connected at last with the importance of town planning and with how transport policy compounds unequal and inadequate access to shops. Who shouts for the poor when planning supermarkets, transport systems and school curricula? It is easier to blame poor diets on financial incompetence.

In the end, *Poverty Bites* is a challenge not just to governments but to us all. We will not be able to maintain pressure on government any government unless we have at our fingertips the right facts, figures and arguments. But be warned as you read it. You are entering the dangerous terrain of trying to address what to do about it. It is not good enough just to moan or remonstrate or study food poverty. We have to act. That is why I applaud the Child Poverty Action Group for publishing this book. It is a return to one of the core issues which sparked the CPAG into existence decades ago.

The realisation of food policy failure has emerged gradually, not least due to dogged campaign co-ordination by non government organisations.[2] But now we have no excuses for not knowing. Ministers cannot be allowed to blame the poor for inadequate diets. Quietly, over recent decades food poverty has crept up the policy agenda. Remember that it was the Conservative Government that set up the Food and Low Income Project Team (LIPT) as part of the Nutrition Task Force.[3] By 1992, in its Health of the Nation White Paper, the Conservatives had recognised that 'variations in health' (that weasel phrase for inequalities) was a real cost drag. They recognised too that this was dangerous policy territory. As members of LIPT, Liz Dowler and I were given terms of reference that excluded any discussion of benefit levels, when everyone knew that was central. Ironically this meant that LIPT could focus on the other issues which were also in serious need of attention issues such as access, availability, range of foods, local action, etc. New terrain was opened up, about the structural not just income characteristics of modern food poverty.[4]

The LIPT reported in 1996 but there was no action from the dying days of the Major Government, and the baton was taken up by the incoming Labour Government's Acheson Inquiry into Inequalities in Health[5] and then the Social Exclusion Unit's Policy Action Team 13 on Access to Shops (a real snappy title that one!).[6] Both these reports underlined the structural dimension underlying food poverty. By this we mean issues such as where supermarkets are sited, the warped payments of the Common Agricultural Policy, inadequacy of income levels, and much more.

As this book demonstrates, food poverty raises many complex questions. But above all, it is a challenge to political priorities. We need to campaign not just to raise benefit levels but also to tax the more affluent. We need to shout loudly that more just societies are healthier societies.[7] Whatever our income or circumstances, the problem of modern food poverty is not the problem of the poor alone. Someone who experiences food poverty, feels it individually of course. It is their stomach, their health that suffers. But the rest of us collude with it structurally if we do not challenge it. The stark fact is that the food revolution of the last half century the new foods, new farming systems, new long-distance logistics is presently in a fair bit of trouble. Britain's national food policies ought to have been seen to be in crisis due to their appalling record of food poverty and inequalities-related ill-health. But the straw that broke their back was not poverty but that the Treasury and politicians' tolerance for farm subsidies was broken by the bills for BSE and foot and mouth disease. The Treasury and European Union has had to fork out nearly £8 billion, all to support farming's right to export. It is sad but true that trade and fiscal interests have been more important than social suffering in bringing food policy to the boil.

As we read this book, we need to remember that over the last half century the food economy has been driven by and structured to suit the more affluent. *Poverty Bites* is a wonderful reminder that the next half century must put the food system on a more sustainable basis and must put the needs of the most vulnerable at the heart of any restructuring. If this does not happen, it will not be a sane or just food policy.

Tim Lang, PhD, FFPHM
Professor of Food Policy and Director of the Centre of Food Policy, Thames Valley University

NOTES

1 T Lang, M Caraher, R Carr-Hill and P Dixon, *Cooking skills and health*, Health Education Authority, 1999
2 Sustain the Alliance for Better Food and Farming publishes an excellent quarterly newsletter on UK food poverty projects and actions: *Let Them Eat Cake*, c/o Sustain, 94 White Lion Street, London N1 9PF
3 DoH, *Low income, food, nutrition and health: strategies for improvement*. Report by the Low Income Project Team for the Nutrition Taskforce, Department of Health, 1996
4 S *Leather, The Making of Modern Malnutrition*, Caroline Walker Trust, 1996
5 D Acheson, *Report of the Independent Inquiry into Inequalities in Health*, The Stationery Office, 1998
6 Social Exclusion Unit, *Improving shopping access for people living in deprived neighbourhoods*. Report of Policy Action Team 13 of the Social Exclusion Unit, Department of Health for the Social Exclusion Unit/Cabinet Office, 1999
7 R G Wilkinson, *Unhealthy Societies: the afflictions of inequality*, Routledge, 1996; M Marmot and R G Wilkinson (eds), The Social Determinants of Health, Oxford University Press, 1999

WHAT IS FOOD POVERTY?

INTRODUCTION

The 1996 World Food Summit affirmed the 'right of everyone to have access to safe and nutritious food' and asserted that poverty was a major cause of food insecurity throughout the world.[1] For many people it comes as a surprise to find that food poverty is a critical issue in Britain and that it affects an increasing proportion of the population. The welfare state and the cheap food policies aimed at ensuring people have sufficient resources to buy enough food have not prevented food poverty. The reality is that there are adults and children who do not have enough to eat or who cannot afford to eat healthily.

There are public and visible signs that food poverty exists within Britain and other industrialised countries. For example, there has been an increase in the systems of direct feeding such as soup kitchens, food banks and other distribution networks in countries such as Britain, Canada, Australia and the United States.[2] In Britain over 10,000 people daily are fed by such schemes. Many of us may have tossed a coin to someone asking for 'spare change please, for a bite to eat'. However, it would be wrong to assume that food poverty is just experienced by the homeless or by others who are 'down in their luck'. Instead, food poverty extends beyond those who live on the streets and exists in the homes of individuals and families throughout the country. Food poverty experienced by households and families was, and continues to be, hidden from view and this partly explains why Lang (1999) described it as a 'Cinderella subject within public policy', one that merited little debate and even less action.

For many years the only formal recognition of food poverty was in terms of the official statistics which showed that sections of the population experienced particular health problems, some of which were nutrition related. Under previous governments the causes and outcomes of food poverty were seen to be the responsibility of individuals who were accused of wasting their money or of ignoring nutritional advice. However, since the New Labour Government came into power in 1997 food poverty has been placed on the policy agenda and many departments are developing policies aimed at tackling this issue. The Deputy Head of the Food Standards Agency has stated that:

> food poverty, is of course a multi-faceted problem. It is partly about sufficient income; it is also about access to shops, knowledge and confidence in food skills, as well as the promotion and advertising of food.[3]

The aim of this book is to contribute to the current debate on food poverty by examining its causes and consequences as well as exploring some of the policy options. The food economy is one of the most dynamic and competitive in our society yet significant proportions of the population are marginalized from it. This book explores why this happens and considers the consequences for individuals and their families. We will review what has been and is being done to address these problems, and highlight some of the real challenges for policy makers, campaigners, researchers and rights workers, and for people in the UK, whether rich or poor.[4]

WHAT IS FOOD POVERTY?

Food poverty has been defined as 'the inability to acquire or consume an adequate quality or sufficient quantity of food in socially acceptable ways, or the uncertainty that one will be able to do so.'[5] Research has consistently shown that nutritional status is related to income; that is, the poorer you are the worse your diet. There is increasing evidence that those who live for long periods on low incomes cannot afford to purchase sufficient basic, appropriate food for a healthy life. And while recognising that access, availability and affordability are important dimensions of food poverty, this definition emphasises that food, and the ways in which it is obtained, also have to be socially acceptable as well as nutritionally adequate.

Food is a general marker of social exclusion and those who are unable to eat in ways that are acceptable to society can also be said to experience food poverty. There are many examples of ways in which individuals and families are excluded from a 'minimum acceptable way of life'. For example, those who find food shopping stressful because they have insufficient money, or because the shops they can reach are inadequately stocked with poor quality or expensive goods, as well as those whose children cannot have a packed lunch similar to that of their friends.

Food is an expression of who a person is, what they are worth and a measure of their ability to provide for their family's basic needs. Food is also a focus for social exchange and a major contributor to health and wellbeing. Health and social behaviour are both compromised in households and communities living on low incomes. The social, cultural and psychological functions of food have to be recognised in assessing basic needs as these can also be aspects of food poverty.

FOOD SECURITY

One way of conceptualising and exploring food poverty is to adopt the approach used by the United Nations and other international agencies who use the term 'food security' to summarise ideas about food access and entitlement. Originally food security referred to the national level, that is whether countries had enough food on average to feed their populations. However, the ideas underpinning food security have developed so that it now operates on a micro level. The needs of communities, households and even individuals have come into the picture, and the ideas and principles are increasingly being used to understand the problems faced by poor people and communities in both developing and developed countries.[6] Box 1.1 shows the key aspects of food security that apply to all countries, including Britain.

The concept of food security can be applied in developed, industrialised countries. It makes clear that solutions to food poverty go beyond welfare transfers or health services to include issues of basic human rights, sustainable development, health inequalities and social inclusion. This is because food security is partly about production and supply: food should be produced and distributed in ways which are sustainable, moral and equitable. Food security is also about economic demand and social value: people should be able to acquire, share and

---

BOX 1.1: **Food security**

Food security means that all people at all times should have physical and economic access to sufficient, affordable, safe and nutritious food necessary and appropriate for a healthy life, and the security of knowing that this access is sustainable in the future. In Britain this means people need:

- access to food – to have enough money, and to be able to reach the kind of shops which stock the foods needed for health at affordable prices;
- to enjoy choice – the food people can buy has to be both safe, and necessary or appropriate for a healthy life and for the culture in which they live;
- freedom from fear – as far as possible people should be free from anxiety about whether they will be able to eat properly.

---

consume the food they need, and which is culturally and socially acceptable, in ways that are not demeaning but uphold human dignity.

Food security analysis is a powerful tool which enables people to examine food poverty in a holistic way, and to trace the issues that policy makers need to tackle, as well as the role for professionals and individuals.

THE CONTEXT: POVERTY AND INEQUALITY IN THE UK

In recent years there has been increased awareness of the growing inequalities within British society; inequalities in health and social experiences as well as in incomes. There is a recognition that such inequalities contribute to social exclusion, which is seen as unacceptable both morally and practically: the health and wellbeing of all members of society are affected by the experiences of those living in the worst deprivation.[7] A number of reports discuss inequalities and policy responses. In health, the Acheson Inquiry into *Inequalities in Health* and the subsequent White Paper, *Saving Lives: Our Healthier Nation*, recognised the role of an inadequate diet, and, more importantly, called for 'policies to increase the availability and accessibility of food stuffs to supply an adequate and affordable diet' (p65) and the 'further development of policies which will ensure adequate retail provision of food to those who are disadvantaged' (p66).[8] The *NHS Plan* also recognised inequalities, and focused on the need to increase fruit and vegetable consumption, through improving their availability and affordability at local levels.[9] Other reports such as *Bringing Britain Together: A strategy for neighbourhood renewal* published by the Social Exclusion Unit called for co-ordinated and intersectoral approaches that work with communities to reduce inequalities and improve health. The implications of these reports in terms of the initiatives they set are discussed in Chapter 5.

WHO ARE THE POOR?

There are many books and articles about poverty and inequality in Britain today. Despite the New Labour Government's pledge to reduce inequality generally and in particular to end child poverty within a decade of its first term, the evidence to date is that the gap between those on the highest and lowest incomes is widening, and that child poverty is persisting. During 2000, almost 14 million people lived in households with incomes of less than £137 a week after housing costs – that is, nearly a quarter of the population.[10] Families with children are more at risk of low incomes, particularly if they are headed by a lone parent, than families without children: Government figures show that 1 in 3 children lives in poverty.

These figures come from a large scale, continuous Government funded survey (*Family Resources Survey*), and give good estimates of inequality, which is how poverty is defined throughout Europe. Another indicator of poverty is to look at receipt of means-tested minimum income benefits such as income support. In early 2001, 3.9 million households were living on this benefit: almost seven million people, or nearly 12 per cent of the population.[11]

Poverty is more than low income, and this book is partly concerned with the wider effects of deprivation and exclusion in relation to food. But the Government and many agencies use income as a proxy indicator of poverty – and for those living on low incomes, not having enough money to manage is a daily experience – so income measures are a good place to start. Government statistics also show that poor households are fairly heterogeneous in terms of who is likely to experience poverty. Poverty is more common among women than men; it is also more likely in households with dependent children, and in households where one or more adults is unemployed, or disabled. The greatest number of people who are poor are the elderly – almost three million of them. In this book we concentrate on the effects on families with dependent children.

Since 1997 the financial situation has improved for families living on benefit because the allowances for children within income support have increased considerably. For example, in 1997 the allowance for a child under 11 was £16.90 and in 2001 it had increased to £24.90. Levels of benefit are still not generous, and do not allow claimants to live luxurious lives: for instance, on current benefit levels families would have just over £5 a person a day for all their needs. Much research over the last two decades has shown that benefit levels are insufficient to enable people to purchase all they need.[12] We examine whether benefit levels are enough to purchase a diet needed for health on p17.

HOW MANY PEOPLE FACE PROBLEMS OF FOOD POVERTY?

The straight answer is that no one knows. There has never been a survey of nutrition and diet in low income households, although the Food Standards Agency, which now has responsibility for commissioning national nutritional surveys, is likely to commission one in 2002. What we do know, however, is that households who live on low incomes, whether from wages or benefits, for more than a few months are unlikely to have enough money to buy the food they need to maintain good health. If they cannot reach the major supermarkets or street markets without incurring additional transport costs as well, they are even less likely to be able to afford essential food.

The numbers of people and households claiming income support in early 2001 is shown in the Table 1.1.

The Zacchaeus Trust and Church Action on Poverty, among others, argue that neither the minimum wage, nor benefit levels (whether income support or pensions) are sufficient to cover food needs. The longer people live on benefits, the less likely the money they receive covers costs. In August 2000, 2.67 million children (20 per cent) were living in a family claiming a key benefit;[13] of these, 60 per cent had been on benefit for at least two years, and for the sick and/or disabled group, the proportion was 74 per cent.[14]

The value of the food element in benefits is not transparent. It is impossible to calculate what benefit rates are intended to cover. In the past, the Department of Social Security sought advice from the Department of Health and Ministry of Agriculture, Fisheries and Food's Nutrition Section (MAFF) over how possible it was to purchase an adequate diet for health on low incomes or benefits. In 1992, as part

TABLE 1.1: **Income support and jobseeker's allowance – numbers of claimants, partners and dependants**

Income support claimants and average amounts: February 2001

Type of household	Numbers claiming amount	Average weekly
lone parents	900,000	£98.86
aged 60+	1,680,000	£46.31
disabled	1,000,000	£72.48
others	310,000	£68.40
all	3,890,000	£66.93

Income support claimants – February 2001
Numbers of partners
558,000

Dependent children aged				
under 5	5-10	11-15	16+	total
675,000	828,000	636,000	154,000	2,294,000

TOTAL NUMBERS DEPENDENT ON INCOME SUPPORT: 6,742,000

Jobseeker's allowance – November 2000
Claimants: 961,000; 730,000 of whom claim income based JSA, and of these, the majority are single or couples with no children. However, 230,000 children depend on JSA, and 140,000 partners.

Source: www.dss.gov.uk (July 2001)

of an internal check, MAFF simulated a low income 'healthy diet' from the *National Food Survey* data; the week's food cost £10 a head. Not only was this in itself probably more than most low income households spent on food, the pattern of food usage it required was completely unrecognisable and impractical, requiring poor consumers to adopt a totally different eating culture from the rest of the population.[15] However, these results were not communicated as showing the inadequacy of benefit levels; rather the reverse – they were deemed to show that, theoretically, benefits were sufficient if people purchased foods 'sensibly and wisely'. In fact, sense and wisdom was what was lacking on the part of those making the judgement.

The food element in benefit levels is not protected or ring-fenced when fines or mandatory deductions are made for debts or arrears; sometimes the household is left without sufficient money to purchase enough food. However, this problem belongs to the household alone: it is no one else's. Agencies responsible for utility and housing costs can recover them from low income households; no agency has responsibility to ensure the household can buy food.

FOOD IS AN IMPORTANT ISSUE

All the evidence shows clearly that a poor diet increases the likelihood that people that people will develop coronary heart disease, non-insulin dependent diabetes, or cancer.[16] They will be ill, which requires treatment which itself costs money, and are more likely to die young. Food poverty and insecurity, while it is experienced by individuals, is also an important issue for all of society. The final section of this chapter considers why food is important to parents, professionals and the general public.

PARENTS

Many parents find contemporary food culture in relation to children a challenge and, for some, a perpetual anxiety. Mealtimes and eating are experienced as a battle, either to get children to eat anything at all, or to persuade them to eat what parents feel is a reasonable, good diet. Many parents are worried that their children only seem to want to eat (what parents describe as) 'junk' food. Although some research shows that older children can be quite sophisticated about advertising and television, many children, particularly the younger ones, are susceptible to the endless bombardment to buy foods that are expensive, high in fat, sugar and salt, and particularly fast foods.[17] Food manufacturers and retailers invest a lot of time and money into raising the profile and appeal of products such as breakfast cereals, yogurts, crisps, biscuits and fizzy drinks, and use subtle marketing devices to promote their purchase.[18] A report by Sustain in June 2001, which updated their previous studies, confirms that TV advertising of food and soft drinks, as a proportion of total TV advertising of all products, is between two and three times higher during children's programming compared to adults', and that advertising for sweets, cakes and biscuits forms the largest category of food advertised on children's TV.[19] Furthermore, the foods advertised were almost universally high in fat and/or sugar and/or salt; there were no advertisements for fruit and vegetables during the survey times. The majority of the foods shown were branded packaged or processed goods. Not all of these are unhealthy, according to current government guidelines, but many were.

For those who are living on tight budgets, the mixture of sophisti-cation required to resist the persuasiveness of adverts, and the anxiety that children cannot or do not, is particularly acute. For instance, many researchers have documented parents (and others) explaining that they buy branded goods, which are sometimes more expensive than store own-brands, because they cannot afford, literally, to make mistakes and buy foods their children will not eat, or which they cannot quite trust to be 'good food'. They may also buy branded goods to use the packaging or container as receptacle for a non-branded product, to disguise their having bought a cheaper, own brand variety. Children in particular can be demanding consumers, and ruthless in picking on and mocking those who do not appear to conform – who drink the 'wrong' type of drink or eat the wrong snacks.[20] What goes in a child's lunch box marks them out as belonging or different; children can be laughed at for being poor if they cannot afford to eat the latest 'fashionable' food. Food can be a marker for social exclusion for children as well as for adults. Food 'choice' for poor parents has to be governed by price and what they can afford, however much they want also to provide what they children want to eat, and what they know they will eat.

Parents (and teachers) face a different set of anxieties over school meals. For many children, schools provide the main meal of the day during term-time, particularly for those who come from low income households. Parents may be, and often are, concerned about the quality and palatability of what is provided, and, if claiming income support, face additional anxieties in that there is no guarantee that what is provided as the free meal is hot food. Secondly, in many schools the experience of eating free meals can be very negative. Children can be stigmatised for having to eat a free meal; they may have to eat it separately from their friends who bring a packed lunch, or don't eat the free meal.[21] Schools are normally sensitive to these issues, including teasing and bullying, but they are not easy to overcome. Children do not always report the teasing so adults in school tend to downplay the embarrassment and problems over eating free school meals.

One of the major issues associated with school meals is that, how-ever well presented the food is and however nutritionally desirable, ultimately the success of the enterprise depends on whether children eat the food provided. Whether they do so or not depends partly on children's reluctance to eat foods that are novel. Many children are conservative in their tastes and need encouragement to try foods that are different from those to which they are accustomed. Children who are vegetarians may be uncertain about whether dishes contain animal products. Others will only eat certain foods if their friends do, particularly foods that are thought to be 'healthy', which are perceived to be boring.[22] Parents know these reactions only too well; low income parents have little scope for ways to encourage experimentation, and have to hope that schools can play their part – a hope often misplaced.

PROFESSIONALS IN HEALTH, EDUCATION AND SOCIAL WORK

Those who work with families who are living on low incomes are aware of the anxieties people have about how they can obtain adequate quality and quantity of food. There is now a much greater awareness of the importance of food for health and wellbeing and relevant professionals (GPs, health visitors, midwives, health promotion workers, community development officers, teachers, social workers) are keen to know how best to address the problems.

In addition, those working to reduce social and health inequalities, whether on the ground or in research, are increasingly aware of the problems of food access. The Government reports referred to above (the public health White Paper *Our Healthier Nation*, the Inquiry into inequalities in health chaired by Sir Donald Acheson, the report from the Social Exclusion Unit on building better neighbourhoods) all mention the problems that low income households face in obtaining access to appropriate, sufficient food for health and wellbeing. A number of local authorities or local health authorities have appointed food poverty officers; Health Action Zone initiatives include activities to address and improve food access. These developments are discussed in more detail in Chapter 5.

However, no Government department has responsibility for ensuring all people have physical and economic access to healthy food at reasonable prices. There is no formal recognition within government of how much minimal but reasonable living costs. The Family Budget Unit reports on the amount of money needed by families with young children or pensioners to be able to live at low cost but acceptable levels have been ignored within Government.[23] The Food Standards Agency may commission more research into the problems faced by low income consumers, but such research has had a very low priority in Government research spending until now.[24] No one has statutory responsibility to ensure that people can reach decent shops. The

Government Inquiry into supermarket monopolies recognised that the practice by major retailers of maintaining cheap prices on 'loss leaders', and the manipulation of local food prices, both damage small local retailers. However, the Inquiry could propose no action to deal with the problem.[25] Meanwhile, families on low incomes have to struggle the best they can with the results of this 'non-joined up' policy making.

GENERAL PUBLIC AND THE MEDIA

The main news about food on TV, radio and in the newspapers is nearly always about food safety and quality, rather than about food and health. This focus is probably because of the major crises which have affected farmers, exports, and consumer safety: foot-and-mouth, BSE/vCJD, salmonella, *E.coli*, and which have therefore dominated news because of the economic impact. As a result, people generally express considerable anxieties about whether the food they eat is safe, about who they can trust, and about how food is grown, imported and processed within the food chain.[26] There has been a wealth of publicity over genetically modified foods and their impact on the environment and on individuals, and there has been some discussion about the retail dominance of the major supermarkets. Concern is also expressed about farming and animal production systems, not least following the 2001 foot and mouth outbreak, as well as over the farming sector itself in the UK.

One response to these anxieties has been an increased demand for organic foods, and for products that have been produced in environmentally sound ways and fairly traded. There is a growth in Farmers' Markets, which sell local produce to local consumers. To some extent these trends are evidence of reactions to the intensive, centrally dominated system of producing and marketing food, and to the intense globalization of food markets. Usually, such issues are discussed separately from those of food security and problems of food access for the poorest in society. This is surely a false distinction. Many who live on low incomes have very little consumer choice: they cannot participate in one of the dynamic, leading sectors in society, which produces, distributes and retails an ever expanding range of foodstuffs. This is part of their social exclusion. What is more, globalization of food production and retailing affects those who are poor in poor countries as well as in rich. All people should be – and should feel – included in discussion of, and strategies for, sustainable, enjoyable food security.

SUMMARY

- Food poverty is the inability to acquire or consume an adequate quality or sufficient quantity of food in socially acceptable ways, or the uncertainty that one will be able to do so; it is thus the opposite of food security.
- Solutions to food poverty must address issues of basic human rights, sustainable development and social inclusion.
- A national objective should be that everyone lives in a state of food security:
  - the food economy should contribute to sustainability, health and equity;
  - all people at all times should have physical and economic access so they can choose sufficient, affordable, safe and nutritious food necessary and appropriate for a healthy life.
- Food poverty potentially affects all who live on low incomes from benefits or low wages for more than a few months.
- Food poverty has not been addressed systematically because no government department has responsibility to ensure people have access to healthy food at reasonable prices.

NOTES

1 Food and Agriculture Organization of the United Nations, *Rome Declaration on World Food Security and World Food Summit Plan of Action*, 13-17th November 1996
2 G Riches, 'Hunger, Food Security and Welfare Politics: Issues and Debates in First World Societies', *Proceedings of the Nutrition Society*, 56, 1a, 1997
3 S Leather, 'Can the Food Standards Agency help combat food poverty?' *Newsletter of the UK Public Health Association*, 4, Summer 2000, p13
4 We do not examine the policies and strategies by the newly devolved territories specifically, but refer to initiatives in Scotland, Wales and Northern Ireland where appropriate.
5 See note 2
6 S Devereux and S Maxwell (eds), *Food Security in Sub-Saharan Africa*, ITDG Publishing, 2001; S Maxwell, 'Food Security: a post-modern perspective', *Food Policy*, 21, 2, 1999, pp155-170
7 R Wilkinson, D Blane and E Brunner (eds), *Health and Social Organization: towards a health policy for the twenty-first century*, Routledge, 1996
8 Department of Health, *Saving Lives: Our Healthier Nation*, Cm 4386, Stationery Office, 1999; D Acheson (Chair), *Report of an Independent Inquiry into Inequalities in Health*, Stationery Office, 1998

9 Department of Health, *The NHS Plan*, Cmd Paper no 4818, Stationery Office, 2000

10 Department for Work and Pensions, *Households Below Average Income*, 2001

11 Department of Social Security, *Income Support: Quarterly Statistical Enquiry*, February 2001

12 I Cole-Hamilton and T Lang, *Tightening Belts*, London Food Commission, 1986; R Cohen, J Coxall, G Craig and A Sadiq-Sangster, *Hardship Britain, being poor in the 1990s*, CPAG, 1992; H Parker with M Nelson, N Oldfield, J Dallison, S Hutton, S Paterakis, H Sutherland and M Thirlwart, *Low Cost but Acceptable: a minimum income standard for the UK*, Policy Press and Zacchaeus Trust, 1998; E Dowler, 'Budgeting for food on a low income: the case of lone parents', *Food Policy*, 22, 5, 1998, pp405–417

13 Income support, jobseeker's allowance, disability living allowance, incapacity benefit, severe disablement allowance, national insurance credits

14 DSS, First Release: client group analysis: Quarterly Bulletin on families with children on key benefits, August 2000. Available at www.dss.gov.uk

15 S Leather, *The making of modern malnutrition: an overview of food poverty in the UK*, The Caroline Walker Trust, 1996

16 Department of Health, *Low Income, Food, Nutrition and Health: Strategies for Improvement*, A Report from the Low Income Project Team to the Nutrition Task Force, 1996; W P T James, M Nelson, A Ralph, and S Leather, 'Socioeceonomic determinants of health: The contribution of nutrition to inequalities in health', *British Medical Journal*, 314, 1997

17 B Young, *Emulation, Fears and Understanding: a review of recent research on children and television advertising*, ITC, 1998

18 G Tansey, T Worsley, *The Food System: a Guide*, Earthscan, 1995

19 Sustain, *TV Dinners: what's being served up by the advertisers*, Sustain, 2001

20 A J M Donkin, *The effects of television advertising and household income on children's food choice*, unpublished PhD thesis, University of Nottingham, 1997; 'Children's food: ten junk products for every healthy one', *The Food Magazine*, April/June 2000, pp11–14

21 P Storey and R Chamberlin, *Improving the take up of free school meals*, Research Report 270, DfEE, 2001

22 N Charles and M Kerr, *Women, Food and Families*, Manchester University Press, 1988; S A Turner, R Levinson, B McLellan Arnold, S Stevenson, A Donkin and E Dowler, 'Healthy Eating in Primary Schools' *Health Education Journal* 59(3), 2000, pp1–15

23 H Parker with M Nelson, N Oldfield, J Dallison, S Hutton, S Paterakis, H Sutherland and M Thirlwart, *Low Cost but Acceptable: a minimum income standard for the UK*, Policy Press and Zacchaeus Trust for the Family Budget Unit, 1998 and 2000

24 *Food Standards Agency News*, July/August 2001, p1

25 Competition Commision, *Supermarkets: a report on the supply of groceries from multiple stores in the United Kingdom*, Stationary Office, 2000

26 RSGB, *Consumer Attitudes to Food Standard: Final Report*, FSA, 2001

2 CAUSES OF FOOD POVERTY

Food poverty is complex and can be caused by a number of factors acting alone or, more usually, in combination. Figure 2.1 shows the many factors that can determine food security for households and individuals in the UK. By and large, the food people eat comes from what they can buy, which in turn depends on what is available locally and what it costs. The skills and resources household members have in preparing food, as well as tastes and expectations, also govern what people buy and choose to eat. Some food is obtained through institutions, such as schools or work canteens; usually people have to buy this food, though sometimes it is subsidised or free, and they may or may not get much choice over what they can eat. Food that is grown by the household nowadays plays a much smaller role in household or individual food and nutrition security, though in some parts of the country, and for some people with access to allotments or vegetable/fruit gardens, it can be important for certain foods. Nutrition security highlights the importance of the *quality* of the food people eat. Some foods contain more vitamins and minerals than others – either because they are more nutrient dense in the natural state, or because they have been grown, or processed, or prepared, in such a way as to maximise or preserve such nutrients as might be in the food in the natural state.

In order to understand why people experience food poverty, we have to consider:

- food affordability – do people have enough money to buy food?
- food access and availability – can people get to shops selling the range of foods needed at reasonable prices?

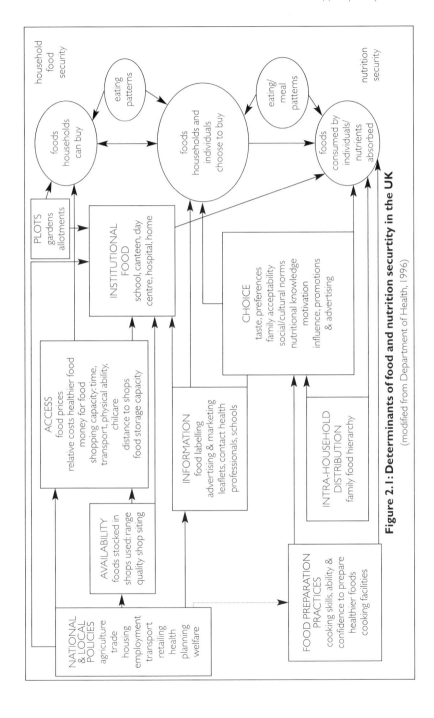

Figure 2.1: Determinants of food and nutrition security in the UK

(modified from Department of Health, 1996)

- food access through institutions – are schools providing appropriate food for children?
- food usage – do people know how to choose appropriate foods and cook them?

Each of these factors is discussed in more detail below. However, for given households and communities, different factors will be more important in shaping their circumstances with respect to food. The context in which the factors occur and interact, as well as how individuals and communities respond to them, are all important in determining the incidence and extent of food poverty. This complexity means there is not always an easy or straightforward explanation for any given household or community as to why they experience food poverty. Equally, there is not one, neat set of solutions that meets all needs.

Figure 2.1 also shows it is important to distinguish households from individuals. Intra-household distributions of both income and wealth, and of access to food, are difficult to study empirically but probably critical in households where both income and food are in short supply.[1]

AFFORDABILITY: DO PEOPLE HAVE ENOUGH MONEY TO BUY FOOD?

There are two ways to answer this question. The first is to cost out a basic standard of living and compare it with incomes of individuals and families who are poor. The second is to ask those who live on the lowest incomes (either from work or benefits) and look at what they actually do in terms of food expenditure and budget management. Both these approaches are described in turn, using recent data, to examine whether or not people can afford the food they need.

COSTING A BASIC STANDARD OF LIVING

There is a long and somewhat controversial tradition of costing a standard of living in the UK, particularly the cost of food, from Seebohm Rowntree onwards.[2] In fact, costing a minimal nutritional component is more difficult and less objective than is often assumed.[3] Usually the approach has been to calculate a theoretical 'least-cost diet': costing the cheapest way of obtaining the minimum necessary nutrients. The problem is that this costs out a diet and a food pattern no one would actually eat, and often entails unrealistic assumptions about both the proportion of income spent on food and the actual food prices obtainable.

An appealing alternative which avoids many of these pitfalls is to use a budget standards approach, applied to food. In this case, basic 'baskets' of foodstuffs, which reflect actual food usage patterns while providing a nutrient content that meets current healthy diet guidelines, are constructed for different household types and costed using typical average food prices. Table 2.1 shows the costs of providing sufficient food for health for a theoretical couple with two children, and a lone parent with two children, using prices from a major supermarket.[4] These calculations were completed by nutritionists using Government data on patterns of food consumption that are characteristic of low income households in the UK, adjusted so they are balanced to promote short and long term health. The acceptability of typical menus that could be constructed from the food budgets were discussed and tested out by families living on low incomes, in different parts of the country.

The cost of purchasing a week's food are higher in households where adult(s) are working outside the home because they are likely to purchase food at work. The costs shown take account of the costs of school meals, where these have to be paid by parents whose children do not qualify for free meals, but not for a household in receipt of income support, whose children would be able to claim free school meals during term time.

Compare the theoretical food costs shown in Table 2.1 with the amount of money similar families would receive in income support, which in 2001 would be £162.65 a week (couple with two children),

TABLE 2.1: **'Low cost but acceptable' – food costs £/week January 1998 prices from a major supermarket and a discount store**

Couple + 2 children (aged 10 and 4 years)		Lone parent family + 2 children (aged 10 and 4 years)	
(2 earners – one part-time)	£61.97	(part-time earner)	£39.25
(no earners)	£57.88	(no earner)	£35.16

The amount of money shown would enable a household to buy enough food to satisfy government healthy eating guidelines, and reference values for intakes of all nutrients, but which is also palatable and acceptable to consumers throughout the UK. For details of the methodology, foods included and typical weeks' menus, see source: H Parker with M Nelson, N Oldfield, J Dallison, S Hutton, S Paterakis, H Sutherland and M Thirlwart, *Low Cost but Acceptable: a minimum income standard for the UK*, Policy Press and Zacchaeus Trust for the Family Budget Unit, 1998. Uprated figures provided by personal communication from N Oldfield, October 2001.

or £132.45 a week (lone parent with two children). Or, compare the food costs shown with the average income a family in the lowest fifth (quintile) of the income distribution, which is about £96 a week.[5] These incomes have to pay for much more than food, and the costs of other basic items such as rent, council tax, gas, electricity and water are outside the household control. People can cut down on usage of gas and water (and often do) if money is tight, but they have to use a large proportion of income to pay for them, as well as for clothes, transport, toiletries, cleaning materials, etc. The amount of money needed to purchase these food baskets would cost a much higher proportion than could possibly be spent from such incomes on food alone.

In fact, costs to many people living on low incomes would in practice be even higher, particularly for food recommended for health (fruit, lean meat, wholemeal bread) because where they live, such food costs more than in the major supermarkets. This cost differential by place and type of shop is described below.

Some people raise objections to using such an approach; they say that it ignores people's choice over what food to buy, and does not allow for ingenuity in cooking and budgeting methods. But budget standards are not meant to be prescriptive: they are not a way of saying to households 'this is how you ought to live to be healthy'. Rather, the method allows us to say, 'given the ways in which average, typical families live, this is the least money different types of household need to spend in order to achieve a given standard of living, and, in the case of food, meet current recommendations for health.' Some researchers modify the methods so that ordinary household members draw up the necessities and cost them. These are known as consensual budget standards. The costs of living they produce are very like those produced by the nutritionists and other professionals shown in Table 2.1.[6]

MEASURING FOOD EXPENDITURE

Looking at the amounts low income households actually spend on food, the annual *Family Expenditure Survey* shows that households in the lowest 10 per cent of the income distribution spend the highest proportion on food than any other group: 21 per cent of their income goes on food, against those in the top 10 per cent who spend 14 per cent on food. However, those in the lowest income category actually spend much less than richer households in absolute terms: in 1999/2000 about £25.20 a week rather than £106.00, which the richest 10 per cent spend. If we look at expenditure on particular types of food, such as fruit, households with incomes below £96 a week spent about £0.20 a week, while households with incomes above £940 a week spent about £4.40 a week on fruit alone – which is about a sixth of what the poorest households spend on all foods.[7] These actual expenditures, measured on typical low income families in national surveys, suggest people are not spending enough money to buy the foods which enable them to eat healthily.

There have been many small studies looking at how low income households spend their money and what they buy. A recent study in Leicester found that families could only afford to spend between £30 and £35 a week to feed a family of four. This equates to £1.16 a person a day for food. A school meal roughly costs £1.28 and the Family Budget Unit estimate (Table 2.1) shows that in theory, such a family would now need to spend at least £61 a week to eat healthily. The families in Leicester would need to spend nearly twice as much to reach even this modest standard.[8]

What happens in reality has been demonstrated in some carefully constructed surveys: people go without. It is not easy to systematically document people's subjective experiences of being hungry, although the United States national survey system does include a food security indicator which tries to do just that.[9] In practice, going without food is not something people find easy to tell survey workers or researchers, so regular, national government surveys are likely to underestimate the incidence. A controversial but important survey in 1991 by the National Children's Home found that one in five parents, and one in ten children, went hungry on a regular basis because they did not have enough money for food. Half the parents in the survey had gone without food to make sure their children had something to eat.[10] More recently, a large national survey of poverty and exclusion found that almost 2 per cent of children did not get three meals a day because there was not enough money, and almost 5 per cent of parents could not afford to provide fruit at least once a day.[11] This was despite parents making huge sacrifices to enable their children to have what they felt was necessary: parents do not deliberately withhold food from their children, nor willingly or happily let them do without. Indeed, the recent national *Family Expenditure Survey* showed that the proportion of food spending that goes towards children is fairly constant across income groups (although, again, the actual, absolute amounts differ). In other words, poorer parents often go without to try to protect their children's diets.

How do people on these low incomes manage to afford the food they do buy? The simple answer is 'with great difficulty'. It is not necessarily that people do not know how to organise their budget, or shop for food properly. Many studies have shown that poor households, in Britain as elsewhere, are skilled at budgeting, and develop careful strategies for reducing expenditure and maximising limited incomes.[12] In practice, expenditure on food is what people often cut to avoid or reduce debts, or meet essential demands: for many it is the only flexible item of their budget. People economise on food either by buying cheaper or different items (no fruit, fewer vegetables, cheaper processed meats), or by omitting meals altogether. Some, who have food in store cupboards, become very skilled and ingenious is preparing low cost but acceptable meals. Others have to resort to borrowing food or money for food.[13] We describe these strategies in more detail in Chapter 4, along with their consequences for health and for people's sense of themselves and their well being.

> I normally buy four packets of bread, [but if I'm running out of money for food] we just buy two. So those who have 6 slices I tell them to take 4, those taking 4 I tell them to take 3 and I don't eat. [...] When we don't have enough, say one boy comes and says, 'Mummy I'm hungry', and I say, 'wait until the others come and we can divide it', or if he's badly hungry I give him a portion and say, 'don't take anymore – the rest has to go to the other children'. He says, 'Mummy trust me'. [...] sometimes I lie to them (then) they say, 'Mummy, don't we know you're are trying to keep us alive, but don't starve yourself, let's share it'. They are very good children, they understand.[14]

FOOD ACCESS AND AVAILABILITY: CAN PEOPLE GET TO DECENT SHOPS?

During the 1980s and 1990s housing and other policies were such that many of the poorest in Britain ended up living in local authority housing in inner cities, especially in the older industrial areas and peri-urban estates, where major sources of employment have closed. Shops and banks have withdrawn, partly because the inhabitants spend little, and partly because of retail concentration in superstores (>25,000 sq.ft) designed primarily for car access on peripheral or out of town sites. Superstores have increased from 457 in 1986 to 1,147 by 1998, whereas the number of independent stores has declined by almost 40 per cent over the same period.[15] Street markets, village shops and specialised high street food shops continue to decline, despite recent regeneration efforts. By 1996/7, large supermarkets had captured about 70 per cent of average food expenditure, including fresh fruit and vegetables, from about 50 per cent in 1991, and this trend is increasing.[16] At the same time, local food retailing has been collapsing, along with small-holding producers. The demise of post offices and banks in rural areas has been widely reported (although little has yet changed by way of solutions) yet the equal loss of shops in rural areas is hardly mentioned.

Shopping journeys by car and the average distance travelled to shops has increased. But the poorest in cities and towns, and sometimes in rural areas, do not have cars; many are unable to walk far with heavy shopping because of physical disability or having young children, and public transport to better shopping centres is often inadequate. The result is that those living in poor areas use discount stores, which carry a limited range of goods and often little fresh produce. When there is an alternative it is often a small local supermarket and corner shops, whose operating margins are such that their food is relatively expensive, and they too may also carry limited ranges of goods. These small shops are vulnerable to closure, particularly if they are in places where banks have withdrawn small local branches and/or where sub-post offices are also under threat. The loss of these amenities also means that even fewer people will use the shops for anything other than small scale top-up shopping. Shops cannot stock fresh produces in such circumstances, and struggle to survive at all.

Recent research in Sandwell, West Midlands, has shown that, in an area of high socio-economic deprivation and where health indicators are also poor:[17]

- there are large networks of streets and estates where no shops selling fresh fruit and/or vegetables exist (or still exist – see figure 2.2);
- there are large networks of streets and estates where such fruit and vegetables as are available in local shops are expensive (see figure 2.2);
- inexpensive, good quality food, including fresh fruit and vegetables, is available only in small, concentrated shopping areas, to which the majority of the population would have to travel by car or public transport;
- small retailers struggle to survive, especially if they try to offer 'healthy' food and perishable goods, against competition from larger stores.

People who live on low incomes do not universally live where shopping facilities are inadequate or depressing – but many do. These

FIGURE 2.2: **Map showing access to shops stocking more than eight reasonably priced fruits or vegetables, in Sandwell, West Midlands**

Legend

— Roads within 500m   ┼┼┼ Railways

— Roads further than 500m   — Canals & streams

★ Postcode containing one or more shop

Reproduced from the (2001, Sandwell, Landline) ordnance survey map by permission of Ordnance Survey on behalf of the controller of Her Majesty's Stationery Office, © Crown Copyright MC100036041
Source: E Dowler et al, Measuring Access to Healthy Food in Sandwell, 2001

problems were recognised by the Social Exclusion Unit in setting up Policy Action Team No.13 (PAT 13), to develop a strategy to increase access to shopping for people in poor neighbourhoods.[18] The PAT 13 report examines the complexity of reasons undermining commercial viability of small independent stores. There is variation from one

BOX 2.1: **Summary of factors contributing to the problems of small independent food stores (taken from PAT 13 report, Department of Health, 1999)**

- **Falling and low local demand**: where there is a shop, people often do not want to use it and, those that can take their spending power elsewhere, do.
- **Crime and the threat of crime**: unsightly security measures and threat of personal safety put customers off using local shops.
- **Competition**: lack of local competition from alternative local convenience stores sometimes leads to overpricing and provides no incentive for improving quality resulting in the provision of poor quality goods.
- **Racism** towards members of ethnic minority groups who run small shops, which damages trust and the commercial environment, and discourages their children from continuing the family traditions.
- **Lack of wholesaling power**: as shops are small independent operators, owners cannot offer the low prices, loss leaders and discounts typical of large chains.

neighbourhood to another, but the principal factors highlighted are shown in Box 2.1. As the report says:

> The once vibrant local shopping centres or neighbourhood stores that provided a safe place for the local community to meet and access a range of services to meet their everyday needs have mostly disappeared. Boarded up small shops on street corners or in small neighbourhood parades, with only the locals knowing which are open for business and which are not, remain. Only people with no other choice shop there. (p2)

The larger retailers put forward the economic argument that they cannot sustain supermarkets in neighbourhoods described as deprived. Such areas might contain as many as 3,000 to 4,000 households with relatively low purchasing power and if retailers cannot construct sufficient parking space to attract significant custom from outside the area, or guarantee a level of internet ordering, they argue the supermarket would not be commercially viable. There is considerable sensitivity among the major retailers, both about contributing to social exclusion and to environmental issues in greenfield site construction, such that they point to new, inner city small stores and supermarkets with pride. However, these stores do not necessarily benefit those who are poor. Generally these new city stores are not located where poorer people live (they are more likely to be where richer people work), or there are not enough of them, and their product range can be limited and more expensive than in the equivalent superstores.

What is clear is that the retailing landscape is changing very fast. It is a highly competitive arena, and several marketing niches are developing.[19] Those with low incomes who spend comparatively little are not an attractive customer base nor do they wield much consumer power. They are also a heterogeneous group in terms of shopping patterns and strategies. They vary in how much time they can spend going from shop to shop in search of bargains, which can depend on how many young children they have to look after, of what age, and partly on whether or not they are disabled or work unsociable hours.

Retailers are more interested in families that have plenty of money, including those who have the time to browse well stocked food shops filled with luxury and exotic lines, and who relish the increase in small specialised, relatively expensive but high quality food shops (delicatessens, bakers, butchers, fishmongers, greengrocers) which have sprung up where better-off people live. Those who are well-off but time-poor make increasing use of internet shopping and high quality ready-prepared foods and meals, and they also eat out of home more and more, in restaurants and bars. The unpalatable truth is that these are the people whose custom and loyalty the major retailers want. The other main type of household they are willing to court are those who do not necessarily have a lot of time and money, but do have enough of both to enjoy shopping, including for food, as 'entertainment'. So, the growth in out-of-town super-shopping malls, where consumers can spend a 'day out', is a response: efficient for the retailers because they streamline costs and attract large numbers prepared to spend and efficient for households as a way of purchasing their needs. Despite much rhetoric, none of the major retailers shows much interest in the problems of low income families.[20]

FOOD AFFORDABILITY: HOW MUCH DO PEOPLE HAVE TO PAY FOR FOOD?

How much people pay for food depends where they shop, where they live, and perhaps even what time of day it is. Food prices vary depending on the type of shop, and the difference in prices can be critical, both to people trying to make a few pounds go further, and to those calculating indices of living costs. Until recently few researched or even acknowledged this area of food poverty.[21] Food is often measurably more expensive in corner shops, convenience stores, and independent small supermarkets than in large or discount supermarkets, for basic 'filling' foods as well as those recommended for a healthy diet (wholemeal products, leaner meat, fresh fruit and vegetables).

In the mid-1990s David Piachaud and Josephine Webb from the London School of Economics measured food prices in a sample of different kinds of shops in an East Midlands county town, and pairs of small shops and supermarkets in five areas around Britain. They found that, on average, basic foodstuffs cost 24 per cent more in small stores than in the big supermarkets, comparing like for like. If they took supermarket 'own brands' into account, the differences in costs were 60 per cent, even without taking special offers or economy brand prices into account. They calculated that a household on benefit would have to spend 25 per cent more of their income on food if they could not get to a large supermarket or street market. The Consumers' Association conducted a survey of shops in 11 different areas around the country. They found that where poorer people lived, the range of foods for sale was fairly limited, with healthy options, such as wholemeal bread or semi-skimmed milk, particularly hard to find, and if present, expensive. A basket of 12 widely available basic foods cost 50 per cent more in local shops (£7.87) than in supermarkets (£5.17). Fruit and vegetables were similar in price, but frozen foods, coffee and tea, bread and breakfast cereals, were twice the price in local shops (see Figure 2.3).[22]

Just noting prices does not give much direct sense of the quality of the food available: whether or not the produce looked fresh and good value for money (for fresh produce); whether or not the tinned or packaged goods' taste was acceptable. These are obviously subjective to some extent (though partly reflected in price). None of the surveys above specifically addressed 'quality' systematically. In the Sandwell study (p21), the field worker made notes on various aspects of food quality and shop hygiene when collecting data on price. These were not used in the maps of reasonably priced shops shown in Figure 2.2, but are being analysed separately.

In Scotland, groups of poor parents got together to make their own price comparisons. Their findings are in Figure 2.4, and they too show how much prices of basic goods varied, depending which shop was used. The cost of a typical shopping basket of basic goods, buying the same foods, could vary by nearly £7, depending whether it was bought in a local shop or in a large supermarket. The prices were collected by local volunteers from 30 different shops.[23]

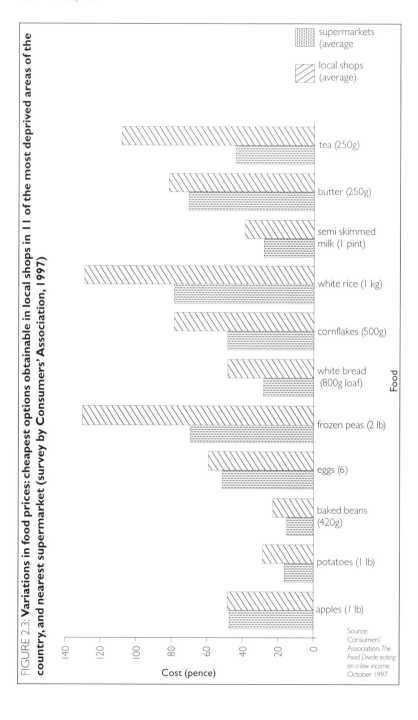

FIGURE 2.3: **Variations in food prices: cheapest options obtainable in local shops in 11 of the most deprived areas of the country, and nearest supermarket (survey by Consumers' Association, 1997)**

supermarkets (average

local shops (average)

tea (250g)

butter (250g)

semi skimmed milk (1 pint)

white rice (1 kg)

cornflakes (500g)

white bread (800g loaf)

frozen peas (2 lb)

eggs (6)

baked beans (420g)

potatoes (1 lb)

apples (1 lb)

Food

Cost (pence)

Source:
Consumers'
Association, *The
Food Divide: eating
on a low income*,
October 1997

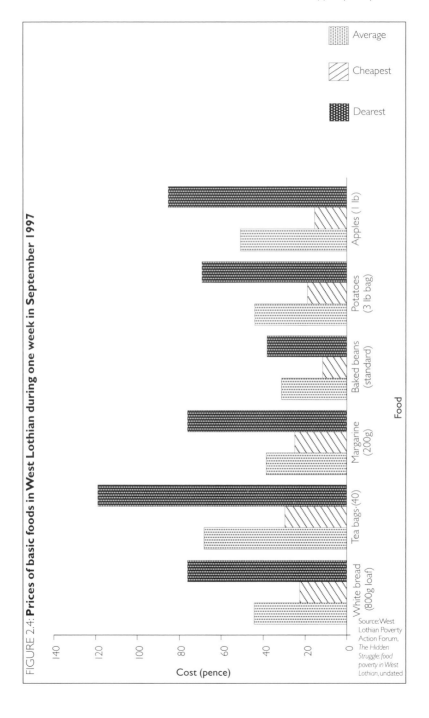

FIGURE 2.4: **Prices of basic foods in West Lothian during one week in September 1997**

Legend:
- Average
- Cheapest
- Dearest

Cost (pence) — axis: 0, 20, 40, 60, 80, 100, 120, 140

Food categories: White bread (800g loaf), Tea bags (40), Margarine (200g), Baked beans (standard), Potatoes (3 lb bag), Apples (1 lb)

Source: West Lothian Poverty Action Forum, *The Hidden Struggle: food poverty in West Lothian*, undated

Money can also be saved by bulk buying, but not all low income households have sufficient cash to be able to do that on a regular basis, and not all can get to places where bulk buying is possible, and carry the purchases home again, without access to a car.

> [...] like buying those tiny little cans because you can't afford the bigger ones.

> (second person) Yes, which costs you more in the long [run]. You can't buy big things of washing powder, you have to buy the 2lbs boxes every week that don't last two minutes. So we pay more out for shopping in the long [run].[24]

Monitoring the price of food in different shops and places is quite a complex business. For instance, supermarkets target special offers at their loyalty card owners. Food items do not necessarily cost the same in the same major supermarket in different parts of the country; prices vary slightly to reflect local store sourcing and running costs (and therefore store size). In some areas, where shop provision is good, food availability can be quite reasonable and prices can be quite low even in small supermarkets and local small stores. This is especially true of those run by Asian and other ethnic minority groups, who often manage to keep operating costs down by using family members for labour.[25]

Such local price variations might be a small proportion of the cost of food for a household on average incomes and hardly noticeable. However, many of those who live on low incomes spend small amounts of money on food, and these variations can be very important. To a family on income support or low wages, £5-10 difference in food costs could account for nearly a fifth of their weekly food bill – which makes the difference between having enough and going hungry. Government surveys estimate that low income households now spend around £15 a person a week on food; earlier we showed smaller in-depth surveys find spending can be as low as £5-£10 a person a week, depending what other expenses are having to be met at the same time. These differences and even the actual amounts may seem small, but low income households can spend a quarter or more of their budgets on food. Such households have very little flexibility in how they spend their money from week to week. Many have little choice but to prioritise payments for rent, gas or electricity. Therefore, having to pay a few pence or pounds extra a week for basic foods because of local shop prices can mean not buying certain items at all. The evidence is that fruit is usually the item that is omitted.

The main thing is price because sometimes you get it 2 pence cheaper. If you calculate 1p is nothing, 5p is nothing but at the end of the day it might come to 50p and that stands for 2 pints of milk. [26]

It is not only food costs that vary with where people live. The Policy Studies Institute showed recently there was marked regional variation in the cost of rent, council tax, utilities (other than food) and domiciliary care. The variations they measured were more than £50 in housing costs, and up to £10 a week for other basics.[27] They calculated that such price variations could absorb up to a fifth of benefit payments for claimants in identical circumstances, depending where they lived. Intra-regional variations were bigger still, especially in the regions with high average costs. No one, as far as we know, is adding the variation in price of food, particularly prices typical of corner shops, to such calculations.

These findings are part of the consequences of privatisation of basic utilities. A recent study, by the School of Architecture, Planning and Landscape at the University of Newcastle upon Tyne, looked at access to energy, telephones, banking and food retailing in two marginalised neighbourhoods. It investigated the effects of privatisation and restructuring of basic services and found that service providers had withdrawn from less affluent neighbourhoods or areas populated by poorer people, even when these were targets of major regeneration activities. All the residents interviewed made a strong connection between poor health and their restricted access to good quality, affordable food and difficulties in heating their homes properly. Few people had bank accounts; this also had implications for basic budgeting and access to other financial services, such as affordable credit. These researchers also measured the costs of using pre-payment meters, small food shops, public telephones or credit agencies, all of which considerably exacerbated the difficulties of managing on a low income.[28]

One consequence of the problems described above is that many people who live for long periods on benefits or low wages get into debt. Sometimes this indebtedness is to government agencies, such as the social fund or housing authorities; sometimes it is to utility companies for arrears in fuel payments; sometimes it is to catalogue companies or other forms of hire purchase; sometimes it is to loan companies or sharks.[29] Whatever the situation, many people cut back on food, particularly when they hit a crisis or demand for a lump sum, prioritising payment to those that can disconnect, fine or imprison a continual defaulter.

FOOD ACCESS THROUGH INSTITUTIONS: ARE SCHOOLS PROVIDING APPROPRIATE FOOD FOR CHILDREN?

Most people have strong opinions about school meals; they are part of the 'folklore' about schools and the shared experience and memories of being at school that go back over many generations. This shared memory is not surprising as school meals have a long tradition in this country. They have always been viewed as important for social, nutritional and educational reasons. Concerns about the health and welfare of children, particularly those from low income households, formed a focus of the original pressures for the introduction of school meals and are still prevalent today. It is worth briefly reviewing school meals now in the context of changes in provision since they were first introduced a hundred years ago.

The Education Act 1906 gave local authorities powers to provide meals for children 'attending an elementary school within their area ... unable by reason of lack of food to take advantage of the education provided for them'.[30] It is ironic and disturbing that almost one hundred years later we still need to provide school meals for some children for the same reasons. National provision of school meals for the majority of children, rather than a minority, was an outcome of wartime provision and legislation when meals, based on minimum nutritional requirements, were provided free to eligible children and at cost price to others. In 1945, the Chief Medical Officer for Health argued that one of the outcomes of wartime rationing and the extension of school meals and school milk provision from 1939 to 1945 was the improved nutritional status of children overall.[31] After the war school meals were continued on a national basis; they were associated with the development of the welfare state and were enshrined in the influential 1944 Education Act. Section 49 of the Act made local education authorities (LEAs) responsible for the provision of milk and school meals for pupils in schools maintained by them. However, the Act went further than the mere provision of meals to a specified minimum nutritional standard, namely one third of the recommended daily intake of calories. School meals were viewed as part of the school day, rather than as an adjunct to the curriculum, providing an important social aspect of school life. The nutritional standards governing school meals continued to be controlled by the Department of Education and Science until the Education Act of 1980 which moved the onus of responsibility for nutritional standards for school meals to LEAs. The devolved responsibility for school meals was less cause for concern than the loss of nationally specified nutrit-

TABLE 2.2: **Cost of a school meal in 12 local authorities, 1999 – random survey by CPAG**

Authority	Primary	Secondary
Worcester	0.84	0.84
Devon	1.15	1.23
Sunderland	1.15	1.15
East Sussex	1.19	1.23
City of Cardiff	1.20	1.30
Edinburgh	1.25	1.80
West Midlands	1.30	1.45
Aberdeen	1.35	1.42
Wandsworth	1.40	1.70
Norfolk	1.40	1.45
Lancashire	1.50	1.60

Source: *Filling the Gap Free: school meals, nutrition and poverty*, CPAG 1999 (p35)

TABLE 2.3: **Range of costs for most popular foods in different schools, 1999 – survey for National Audit Office report on catering in grant maintained schools**

	Price range in pence	Variation (%)	Average price in pence
Pizza	40-70	75	52
Cheese and onion pasty	45-73	62	54
Quiche	40-90	125	60
Chicken and mushroom pie	50-75	50	60
Sausage roll	35-45	29	42
Chipped potatoes	40-65	63	50
Baked beans	18-30	67	23
Cheese sandwich	60-80	33	67
Cola	40-50	25	44
Orange juice	30-45	50	38
Crisps	22-30	36	25

- In schools where catering was contracted-out the price of a two-course meal (main course with potatoes and vegetable, hot or cold sweet and drink) varied from £1.40 to £2.20.
- In schools where catering was provided in-house, price of meal varied from £1.10 to £2.00.

Source: *Filling the gap: free school meal, nutrition and poverty*, CPAG 1999 (p37)

ional standards. LEAs were no longer required to meet nutritional standards for meals or to provide a 'set meal' for pupils, although many continued to do so, basing their policies and guidelines on national guidelines from NACNE and COMA.[32] The social service element continued in that school meals were provided free for children deemed to be 'in need'. The meals provided for these children were the same as for other children in the school. Further concerns about school meals provision were linked to the move to compulsory competitive tendering and to schools moving out of LEA control, during the 1990s. In many instances outside caterers have replaced LEA direct service organisations in providing food in schools and this fragmentation of the service means it is more difficult to monitor food provision in schools overall. What is more, a growing number of authorities provided meals only for those children entitled to a free school meal (other children have to bring a packed lunch) – further stigmatising those who are poor.

A further factor that affected the provision of school meals during the late 1980s and 1990s was the Social Security Act (1986) which came into operation in 1988. One important consequence was that families receiving family credit (the renamed family income supplement, now working families' tax credit) were no longer entitled to free school meals. The entitlement was replaced by a notional amount included in the benefit payment which was in fact insufficient to cover the cost of lunches at school. Until the introduction of the Act, LEAs had had the discretionary power to remit part or all of the charge for school meals and milk; from 1988 they had to charge cost price unless parents received income support. This change in legislation resulted in over half a million children losing their entitlement to free school meals.[33] Nonetheless, about a third of the school population nationally continued to be entitled to free school meals.

Since 1980 there has been continuous pressure on the government from parents, teachers and professional organisations for nutritional standards for school meals to be reintroduced. The school lunch is a very important source of nutrients and, in theory at least, provides variety in the diet, especially for children from poorer families whose diets may otherwise be quite limited.[34] The new Government has taken these issues seriously, and has introduced nutritional standards for school lunches, covering provision for under fives in nurseries as well as for pupils during the compulsory years of schooling from 5 to 16 years.[35] These standards are food based, and do not ban the use of individual foods (such as chips) in school lunches. Secondary schools will have to offer all pupils a balanced food selection but pupils will be free to choose any item or combination of items. Since September 2000 all schools have to provide lunches for pupils who want them – something that has not been a requirement since 1980, although LEAs have had to ensure provision of food for those entitled to a free school meal.

These nutritional standards, while welcomed, have been criticised as not going far enough, and for not being nutrient based and therefore more difficult to monitor. The real challenge, some say, is in ensuring young people make appropriate selections, and actually eat the food provided. This is true for all children, but particularly the case for those entitled to free school meals: up to 20 per cent of children who are entitled to a free school meal do not eat them.[36] There are considerable variations between different authorities. Recent research by the Thomas Coram Institute for CPAG on behalf of the DfEE shows that the stigma attached to school meals, the quality and choice of food, and the way meals are managed, were the key factors.

> Kids whose parents don't have much money are forced to go to the cheap shops and if anyone sees them then they get picked on in the estate and at school. My friend and I have both had these problems. You also get picked on in school if you get a free school dinner ticket, you get called things like poor boy, scavenger and things that are a bit rude and I'm not allowed to repeat. This makes us feel sad and sometimes angry with them and then we get into trouble and get called troublemakers by teachers, which makes it worse.

> *14 year old boy speaking at the All Party Group on Poverty in the Houses of Parliament in February 1999* [37]

The choices on offer in secondary school cafeterias in particular were described as unappealing, with unhealthy options and a restricted, repetitive range of foods on offer. Vegetarians and children following special dietary regimes for cultural, religious or health reasons often found their choice very restricted. Also, the monetary value of the free school meal was too low to provide a well balanced two course meal, and often left children hungry unless they filled up on chips. Where free provision was a packed lunch it was even less popular with children and parents, both of whom hated having no choice over what was in the sandwiches.[38]

Eating is a social experience. We like to eat with friends and sharing food is frequently a sign of friendship – one that children undertake every day. School lunches should be social occasions, with food eaten in a leisurely way in pleasant surroundings. Too frequently this is not the case. And it is certainly not the case for children having to queue for a free school lunch while their friends are eating their own, home produced sandwiches.

Disappointingly, the new guidance on school meals makes no mention of the provision of free school milk to eligible pupils and no encouragement to participate in the EC school milk scheme. Milk could be a valuable dietary supplement for children from poorer households. Also, despite intense lobbying by CPAG and others, the new guidance still does not re-instate the entitlement to free school meals for all low income children, such as those on working families' tax credit, whose entitlement was lost as a result of the 1986 Social Security Act. CPAG estimates that a further 1 million children should be entitled to a free meal in addition to the 2.8 million who are already eligible for such entitlement.[39]

FOOD USAGE: DO PEOPLE KNOW HOW TO COOK?

There is considerable popular anxiety about cooking skills. On the one hand, television programmes and books about cooking or recipes have never been more popular. On the other, surveys suggest fewer of us actually spend much time preparing food on a regular basis. We might make an effort for special occasions, or for a weekly meal together (eg, Sunday lunch), but most of us choose to spend no more than 15-20 minutes preparing the average meal. Many take much less time: they put a frozen 'ready meal' into a microwave for 5-6 minutes, and decant on to a plate (sometimes). Indeed, some argue that traditional cooking skills are becoming redundant as more of us eat convenience food, or eat outside the home, and food manufacturers and retailers have responded rapidly to enable us to do so.[40]

There has not been much research on cooking skills, but there is no evidence that those who are poor are worse than the wider population.[41] Many who live on low incomes are imaginative and resourceful cooks. However, others lack the confidence or the resources to try out new foods when they cannot afford an alternative if family members will not eat the results. Some are understandably nervous of wasting fuel; many do not own the necessary utensils (knives, whisks, bowls, baking trays, casseroles, large saucepans). The evidence suggests that families living on low incomes often rely on convenience foods. This is partly for the same reasons as the rest of the population (the foods can be prepared easily and are popular with children) but also because these foods are relatively cheap, acceptable and reliable with no waste and regular portion sizes.

I mean the point is that the fuel cost, the electricity and gas charges are so high that people can't afford to put their ovens on to do stew and dumplings.

(Second person) Turn of the century they had coal fires that heated the house, you cooked your food on it. Now they're separate.[42]

SUMMARY

- The causes of food poverty are complex and depend on a combination of household and environmental factors. The interaction between local context and circumstances, and responses by individuals and communities to them, is important in determining the incidence and depth of poverty.
- Crucial factors are usually that people living on benefits or low wages:
  - often do not have enough money for food after paying for other essentials (fuel and rent) or where deductions for arrears are made;
  - often live in places where the range of foodstuffs in local shops, and where transport to the major supermarkets, are limited;
  - often have to pay higher prices for food if they cannot reach the major supermarkets or street markets;
  - are often offered limited or inadequate food through schools, and face stigma and anxiety in taking up entitlement to free meals;
  - cannot afford to experiment with preparing or cooking unfamiliar foods, and often have no cooking pots or utensils, or money for fuel.
- Food poverty is experienced in different ways by different people.

NOTES

1   E Dowler, 'Women, food and low income: a cause for concern?' *Health Visitor*, 69, 9, 1996, pp359-3; J Goode, C Callender and R Lister, *Purse or wallet? Gender inequalities and income distribution within families on benefit*, Policy Studies Institute, 1998

2   E Dowler and S Leather, 'Spare some change for a bite to eat? From primary poverty to social exclusion: the role of nutrition and food', in J Bradshaw and R Sainsbury (eds), *Experiencing Poverty*, Vol 3, Ashgate, 2000

3   E Dowler and B Dobson, 'Nutrition and Poverty in Europe: an overview', *Proceedings of the Nutrition Society*, 56, 1997, pp51-62

4　H Parker with M Nelson, N Oldfield, J Dallison, S Hutton, S Paterakis, H Sutherland and M Thirlwart, *Low Cost but Acceptable: a minimum income standard for the UK*, Policy Press and Zacchaeus Trust for the Family Budget Unit, 1998

5　Office for National Statistics, *Family Spending: a report on the 1999-2000 Family Expenditure Survey*, Stationery Office, 2001

6　S Middleton, K Ashworth and R Walker, *Family Fortunes*, CPAG, 1994

7　Office for National Statistics, *Family Spending: a report on the 1999-2000 Family Expenditure Survey*, Stationery Office, 2001

8　B Dobson, K Kellard with D Talbot, *A Recipe for Success? An Evaluation of a Community Food Project*, University of Loughborough: Centre for Research in Social Policy, 2000

9　M Andrews, M Nord, G Bickel and S Carlson, *Household Food Security in the United States 1999*, Food and Rural Economics Division, Economic Research Service, US Department of Agriculture, Food Assistance and Nutrition Research Report No. 8 (FANRR-8), 2000

10 National Children's Home, *NCH Poverty and Nutrition Survey (1991)*, National Children's Home, 1991

11 D Gordon, L Adelman, K Ashworth, J Bradshaw, R Levitas, S Middleton, C Pantazis, D Patsios, S Payne, P Townsend and J Williams, *Poverty and Social Exclusion in Britain*, Joseph Rowntree Foundation, 2000

12 E Kempson, A Bryson and K Rowlingson, *Hard Times: how poor families make ends meet*, Policy Studies Institute, 1994; E Kempson, *Life on a low income*, Joseph Rowntree Foundation, 1996

13 B Dobson, A Beardsworth, T Keil, and R Walker, *Diet, Choice and Poverty: social, cultural and nutritional aspects of food consumption among low income families*, Family Policy Studies Centre with the Joseph Rowntree Foundation, 1994; E Dowler, 'Budgeting for food on a low income: the case of lone parents', *Food Policy*, 22, 5, 1998, pp405–417

14 Lone parent, aged 40+ years, claiming income support with dependent and non-dependent, unemployed children living at home; quoted in E Dowler, 'Families and food poverty' in: N Donovan, C Street (eds), *Fit for School: how breakfast clubs meet health, education and childcare needs*, New Policy Institute, 1999, p31

15 Competition Commission, *Supermarkets: a report on the supply of groceries from multiple stores in the United Kingdom*, Cm4842, Stationery Office, 2000; Department of Health, *Improving shopping access for people living in deprived neighbourhoods*, A Paper for Discussion, Policy Action Team: 13, National Strategy for Neighbourhood Renewal, Department of Health, 1999

16 Department of Health, *Low Income, Food, Nutrition and Health: strategies for Improvement*, A Report from the Low Income Project Team to the Nutrition Task Force, Department of Health, 1996; Department of Health, *Improving shopping access for people living in deprived neighbourhoods*, A Paper for Discussion, Policy Action Team: 13, National Strategy for Neighbourhood

Renewal, Department of Health, 1999

17 E Dowler, A Blair, D Rex, A Donkin and C Grundy, *Mapping access to healthy food in Sandwell*, Report to the Health Action Zone, June 2001

18 Social Exclusion Unit, *Bringing Britain together: a national strategy for neighbourhood renewal*, Stationery Office, 1998; also on www.open.gov.uk

19 M Harrison, C Hitchman, I Christie and T Lang, *Running on empty*, Demos, forthcoming. These issues are elaborated in some detail, with potential policy response.

20 See note 15

21 Local health and community workers have long been aware of the problem. For published work, see J Milburn, A Clarke and F Smith, *Nae Bread*, Health Education Department, Argyll and Clyde Health Board, 1987; *NCH Poverty and Nutrition Survey (1991)*, National Children's Home, 1991; Consumers' Association, *The Food Divide: eating on a low income*, Consumers' Association Policy Paper, October 1997; D Piachaud and J Webb, *The price of food: missing out on mass consumption*, STICERD, London School of Economics, 1996

22 Consumers' Association, *The Food Divide: eating on a low income*, Consumers' Association Policy Paper, October 1997; 'A healthy diet: only all right for some?' *Health Which?* October 1997, pp162-165

23 West Lothian Poverty Action Forum, *The Hidden Struggle: food poverty in West Lothian*, West Lothian Poverty Action Forum, 36 King Street, Bathgate, undated

24 Group of lone parents in Yorkshire, commenting on budgeting on a low income, quoted in P Beresford, D Green, R Lister and K Woodard, *Poverty First Hand: poor people speak for themselves*, CPAG, 1999, p123

25 A J M Donkin, E Dowler, S Stevenson and S Turner, 'Mapping access to food at a local level', *British Food Journal*, 101, 7, 1999, pp554-564; S Cummins and S Macintyre, 'The location of food stores in urban areas: a case study in Glasgow', *British Food Journal*, 101, 7, 1999, pp545-553

26 Lone parent quoted in E Dowler and C Calvert, *Nutrition and Diet in Lone-Parent Families in London*, Family Policy Studies Centre with the Joseph Rowntree Foundation, 1995

27 E Kempson and F Bennet, *Local Living Costs*, Policy Studies Institute, 1997. The difference between the highest and lowest private rent was £115 a week; for council rent the difference was £63 a week; council tax differences were £13.68 a week for band D.

28 S Speak and S Graham, *Service not included: Social implications of private sector service restructuring in marginalised neighbourhoods*, Policy Press for the Joseph Rowntree Foundation, 2000

29 DSS Analytical Division; NACAB, *Make or Break? CAB evidence on deductions from benefit*, E/3/93, National Association of Citizens Advice Bureaux, 1993; P Beresford, D Green, R Lister and K Woodard, *Poverty First Hand: poor people speak for themselves*, CPAG, 1999; J Ford, *Consuming Credit: debt and poverty in the UK*, CPAG, 1991

30 W McMahon and T Marsh, *Filling the gap – free school meals, nutrition and poverty*, CPAG, 1999

31 Ministry of Health, *On the State of Public Health During Six Years of War*, Report of the Chief Medical Officer of Health, 1939-45 (Sir William Jameson), HMSO, 1945

32 A Coles and S A Turner, *Catering for Healthy Eating in Schools*, Health Education Authority, 1993; National Advisory Council on Nutrition Education (NACNE), *Proposals on Nutritional Guidelines for Health Education in Britain: a discussion paper*, Health Education Council, 1983; Committee on Medical Aspects of Food (COMA), *Diet and Cardiovascular Disease*, HMSO, 1984

33 See note 30

34 Department of Health, *The Diets of British Schoolchildren*, HMSO, 1989

35 Department for Education and Employment, *Healthy school lunch guidance for school caterers on implementing national nutrition standards*, DfEE, 2000

36 S Brighouse, *Free School Meals – entitlement vs uptake*, paper presented at Food in Schools Conference, 11 July 2000, London

37 See note 30

38 P Storey and R Chamberlin, *Improving the take up of free school meals*, Research Report 270, DfEE, 2001

39 See note 30

40 T Lang, P Dixon, M Caraher and R Carr-Hill, *The Contribution of Cooking to Health Inequalities*, Health Education Authority, 1999

41 T Lang, P Dixon, M Caraher and R Carr-Hill, *The contribution of Cooking to Health Inequalities*, Health Education Authority, 1999; E Dowler and C Calvert, *Nutrition and Diet in Lone Parent Families in London*, Family Policy Studies Centre with the Joseph Rowntree Foundation, 1995

42 Members of a women's educational project, quoted in P Beresford, D Green, R Lister and K Woodard, *Poverty First Hand: poor people speak for themselves*, CPAG, 1999, p123

3

HOW DOES FOOD POVERTY AFFECT FAMILIES AND CHILDREN?

THE FOOD SYSTEM AND NUTRITION/HEALTH OUTCOMES

Food plays an important part in a person's health, both in the short and the long term. Food patterns and nutrients eaten contribute to health outcomes, such as growth of infants and children, adult body size, and ill health or disease. Data on foods and nutrients are used as indicators of wellbeing, both of individuals and of the society they live in. Where food and nutrient intakes are restricted or inadequate we might expect to see negative consequences in terms of diseases such as coronary heart disease, cancers or reduced resistance to infection, as well as conditions known to be directly diet related, such as iron-deficiency anaemia. We might also look to longer term outcomes such as birthweight, attained height in adulthood (which is associated with good health and longevity) and obesity.[1]

The food system diagram on p15 illustrates the complexity of factors affecting the food choices of households and individuals. On the right of Figure 2.1 are the key outputs of the food system which can be measured in households and individuals: the foods they eat and the nutrients they are likely to obtain. The food coming into the household is regularly measured by government. It is much more difficult to measure reliably and regularly the food and nutrients that individual household members eat. We summarise below the survey evidence that does exist on food patterns and nutrient intakes by different age and gender groups, as well as data on birthweight, child growth and adult body size. We also review the likely impact on the health of parents and their children. We begin by reviewing how to judge the adequacy of someone's food intake.

However, statistics and their professional interpretation are only part of the story. Chapter 4 includes summaries of parents' and children's own experience of the consequences of food poverty, using their own words.

HOW DO WE KNOW WHETHER A DIET IS ADEQUATE OR NOT?

People generally eat many different types of food, in different combinations. There is increasing evidence that eating a range of foodstuffs is good for long term health. Most people know that the consequences of not eating enough food or of eating a very restricted diet lead to classic deficiency diseases, or to general debilitation; to inadequate growth and development in children, and eventually, premature death. But good nutrition is not only fundamental for basic growth and survival; it is also critical for most metabolic functions, including the immune system. Dietary deficiencies can affect short-term health, increasing the risk of dental problems, anaemia and obesity. In the long term, poor diet may increase the risk of coronary heart disease, strokes, osteoporosis and diabetes.[2] There is growing evidence that many cancers are related to a low intake of fresh fruit and vegetables. There is also increasing evidence that a mother's nutritional status, which in turn probably depends on what she ate and how much exercise she took when she herself was a child or teenager, has a long term impact on her baby's health in the womb, soon after birth and throughout that child's life.[3] Nutritional effects last across generations.

Table 3.1 lists the diseases and health conditions seen more commonly in lower socio-economic classes in the UK and the potential role of nutrition and diet.[4] Most of the conditions listed are caused by many factors interacting in complex and, until recently, poorly understood pathways. Smoking is known to be an important contributor to poor health and premature death, and to many of the conditions listed in Table 3.1, but its effect is partly mediated through diet. Smokers tend to eat a different diet from non-smokers, and particularly to eat less fruit, and they probably have higher requirements for many vitamins and minerals to maintain their metabolic repair capacity (known as 'anti-oxidants'). Unfortunately, many smokers in fact have lower intakes of these same vitamins and minerals. Since many smokers are also poor, their health outcome is doubly damaged: they can less afford the fruit and vegetables they need to counter the damaging effects of smoking.[5]

TABLE 3.1: **Excess disease rates in lower socioeconomic classes and their relation to diet in Britain**[6]

Excess disease	Risk factors	Dietary contributors
Anaemia of pregnancy	Low iron; folate status	Low intake of vegetables and fruit; low intake of meat; physical inactivity
Premature delivery	Lower folate; lack of n-3 fatty acids	Low intake of vegetables, fruit, and appropriate oils and fish
Low birthweight or disproportion	Adolescent pregnancy; lower folate; lack of n-3 fatty acids; low weight gain in pregnancy; smoking	Low intake of vegetables, fruit
Anaemia in children and adults	Iron; folate; vitamin C and B-12 deficiency	Possibly premature use of cow's milk; low intake of vegetables and fruit; low intake of meat; diet low in nutrients, with low intake linked to physical inactivity
Dental disease	Low fluoride content of drinking water	Sweet snacks and drinks between meals
Eczema/asthma	Parental smoking; air pollution	Low breastfeeding rates
Insulin dependent diabetes mellitus	Viral infections	Low breastfeeding rates
Obesity in childhood and adults	Poor recreational facilities; intense traffic; excessive television watching; advertising & marketing of foods to children	Physical inactivity; energy dense (high fat) diets
Hypertension	Processed foods; low birthweight; adult weight gain	Salty, energy dense foods with high sodium and low potassium, magnesium, and calcium content; alcohol; low intake of vegetables and fruit; inactivity

Lipid abnormalities

Excess disease	Risk factors	Dietary contributors
High cholesterol	Excess weight gain	Excess saturated fats and some (hydrogenated) vegetable oils
Low high density lipoprotein or high triglycerides	Excess weight gain	Physical inactivity; energy dense diets

Non-insulin dependent diabetes	Excess weight gain	Physical inactivity; energy dense diets
Coronary artery disease	Hypertension; lipid abnormalities; smoking; low folate and antioxidants	Salty, energy dense foods with high sodium and low potassium, magnesium, calcium; alcohol; poor intake of vegetables, fruit and fish; low activity
Peripheral vascular disease	Smoking; low folate; lipid abnormalities	Poor intake of vegetables and fruit and possibly fish
Cerebrovascular disease	Hypertension; low folate; high cholesterol	Salty, energy dense foods high in sodium and low in magnesium, calcium, potassium; alcohol; low vegetable and fruit intake
Cancers: lung, stomach, oropharyngeal, oesophagus	Smoking with excess alcohol intake	Low intake of vegetables and fruit
Bone disease in elderly people	Vitamin D deficiency; confined living and travel opportunities	Physical inactivity, calcium poor diet

Source: W P T James, M Nelson, A Ralph and S Leather, 'Socioeconomic determinants of health: The contribution of nutrition to inequalities in health', *British Medical Journal* 314, 1997, pp1545-9 (with permission from the BMJ Publishing Group)

Traditionally, a person's diet is assessed by looking at the nutrients and other constituents of the foods they eat, and comparing them to reference values. Reference values (which include Reference Nutrient Intakes and Safe Levels, collectively known as Dietary Reference Values) are not recommendations, as in 'everyone ought to eat this much to be healthy, and if you eat less you are malnourished'. Rather, they are used to judge the likelihood that a group of people of a given age are eating enough of a nutrient to avoid deficiency. Alternatively, for some food components, such as saturated fat or salt, they can be used to indicate whether populations are eating more than is associated with good health and a longer life. In the UK, the Dietary Reference Values were published by the Department of Health, and were the work of expert panels of the Committee on Medical Aspects of Food Policy (COMA).[7]

The Dietary Reference Values (DRVs) were used in all the surveys described below to assess the quality of the diets. The reference intakes used in the UK do not yet take account of newer understanding about the protective role of nutrients against cancers and coronary heart disease, nor are they premised on ideas about optimal diets. It could well be that the consequences for longer-term health are more serious still than is implied by the findings linked to current reference values.

More recently, the Department of Health has issued food-based dietary guidelines drawing on recent research, such as recommending people to eat at least five portions of fruit and vegetables a day, with plenty of 'complex carbohydrates' such as bread and pasta.[8] One example of such advice is shown in Figure 3.1. These guidelines are usually used in health promotion, sometimes in hospitals, and in drawing up plans for school meals. They are intended to encourage change, not to judge 'daily' intakes, although some researchers have used them to construct simple 'healthy diet' indicators to try and assess the balance and choices people make about food. These indicators are often used in conjunction with 'food frequency questionnaires', which, as the name suggests, ask people how often they eat different foodstuffs listed by the researcher, rather than asking them to record, in varying detail, what they actually eat over a given period. Healthy diet indicators are useful in that they are easier for non professionals to interpret, and can give general pointers about

FIGURE 3.1: **Balance of good health**

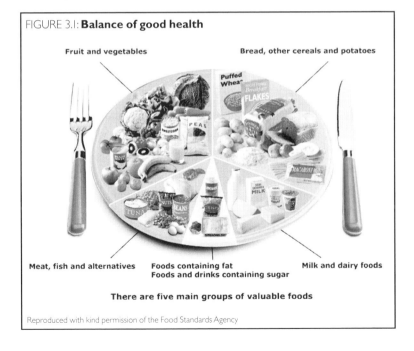

Fruit and vegetables

Bread, other cereals and potatoes

Meat, fish and alternatives

Foods containing fat
Foods and drinks containing sugar

Milk and dairy foods

There are five main groups of valuable foods

Reproduced with kind permission of the Food Standards Agency people's diets, but they are often not validated, quantified indicators of future health or the likelihood of disease. They do not carry the same predictive capacity as reference values.

POOR FAMILIES' FOOD PATTERNS AND NUTRIENT INTAKES

There has not a been national survey of food and nutrition in low income households since John Boyd Orr's seminal study in the early 1930s, a publication which stirred much controversy about how much money people needed to live on.[9] Instead, researchers have used regular and one-off national surveys, and have had to make what sense they can of the food patterns and nutrient intakes of households identified as 'poor' through social indicators such as receipt of means-tested benefits, or social class based on occupation.[10] There have also been some small-scale surveys specifically of households living on low income, or likely to be poor (such as benefit recipients, lone parents, etc).

The current main sources of information about food and nutrient intakes in Britain come from the following sources:

• **National Food Survey**, carried out annually by the Ministry of Agriculture, Fisheries and Food (MAFF) and published by The Stationery Office. A representative sample of about 6,000 house-holds keep a record of food brought into the home for a week; about half detail food eaten outside the home as well. The published reports include money spent, types of food eaten, and nutrients/head calculated from these household data, by region, household type, and by seven income bands and old age pen-sioners. The lowest income bands, for households with or without earners, with gross weekly income below £165 (in 1999; the cut-off was £160 in 1998, and lower in earlier years) can be used to identify low income families. Short-term unemployed households (unemployed less than a year) are classified as 'earners with less than £165 week'.[11]

• **National Diet and Nutrition Surveys**, commissioned by MAFF and the Department of Health (now by the Food Standards Agency) and carried out approximately every three years. Each is a cross-sectional survey of about 2,000 individuals in a particular age group: adults, older adults, school children and pre-school children/ infants. Data are published on food patterns and nutrient intakes, body weight and height, and blood levels of nutrients, measured in individuals (usually the food is weighed and recorded before eating; sometimes food frequency questionnaires are used instead).[12]

- **The Scottish Heart Health Survey**, the **National Child Development Study** and the regular **Health Survey for England**, have food frequency questionnaire data in some rounds of data collection. General food patterns and nutrients/head are calculated from these questionnaires.[13]
- Many smaller scale surveys, sometimes of the general population in a particular area, and sometimes of a particular age or social group, are carried out by research teams. These data are usually published in reports for funders and in academic journals.[14]

FOOD PATTERNS

The surveys described above show fairly consistently that, however 'poor families' are identified, they are likely to consume:

- less fruit juice or fruit, fewer fresh vegetables;
- less semi-skimmed milk, lean meat, oily fish, wholemeal products;
- fewer salads;
- more white bread, potatoes;
- cheaper fatty meats and meat products;
- more beans, eggs and chips,

than richer families. Some of these foods can be crudely classed as 'unhealthy' and to be avoided for a healthy, longer life.

For instance, the table shows the patterns of foods eaten by children aged between one and a half and 18 years old, from two different national surveys, published in 1995 (younger children) and 2000 (older children). 'Poorer children' are defined by being in a household in receipt of benefits, or being in a household where the head is unemployed. Not all the foods that poorer children were more likely to eat are 'unhealthy', but many were. Poorer children were much less likely to eat the foods recommended for a healthy life, such as higher-fibre foods (including fruit and vegetables) and more likely to eat foods with more sugar, starch and sodium than is desirable. The most obvious health consequences are a higher rate of dental caries and slower recovery from infection.[15] Children who eat more sweets are also less likely to eat a varied diet, both when very young and as they grow and develop their own tastes.[16]

TABLE 3.2: **National survey data for children aged 1¹/₂- 4¹/₂ yrs (published 1995) and 4-18 yrs (published 2000)**

Poorer young children more often ate:	Poorer young children less often ate:
white bread	wholemeal bread
sweet/low fibre breakfast cereals	wholemeal, high fibre cereals
margarine, low fat spreads	butter, polyunsaturated margarine
meat pies and pastries	chicken and turkey
chips, crisps	fish
table sugar, sweets	salad, raw vegetables
tea and coffee	fruit, fruit juice

• There were few differences by age.

Poorer older children more often ate:	Poorer older children less often ate (especially boys):
white bread	fruit, fruit juices
whole milk	raw and salad vegetables
meat pies and pastries	bacon, ham
sugar	cheese, cream, butter
	semi-skimmed milk, dairy desserts
	beer, lager, wine, fizzy drinks
	bottled water

• Generally low intakes of fruit and vegetables: 1 in 5 ate no fruit during survey; younger children ate four times the weight of biscuits as green vegetables.

Sources: J R Gregory, D L Collins, P S W Davies, J M Hughes & P C Clarke, *National Diet and Nutrition Survey: children aged 1.5 to 4.5 years,* HMSO, 1995; J R Gregory, *National Diet and Nutrition Survey: young people aged 4-18 years Vol. 1 Report of the diet and nutrition survey,* The Stationery Office, 2000

The National Food Survey data are collected and published every year, so that trends in food consumption and differences between income groups can be identified. Table 3.3 shows how much fresh fruit and vegetables households consumed in the highest and lowest income groups, in 1979 and 1999. The figures include fruit juice consumption, and all fresh green and other vegetables. They exclude fresh and dried potatoes. It is very striking that the differences between the income groups have got wider over the 20 years, particularly for fresh fruit and fruit juice. These measured data from a national government survey reflects what people living on low incomes say in interviews: fresh fruit

TABLE 3.3: **Food consumption and nutrient intake for high (A) and low (D and E2) income groups (from National Food Survey, 1979-99)**

Income group	Consumption in 1979	1999	Difference (1999–1979)
Total fresh vegetables (oz/person/week):*			
A	28.2	30.8	**+ 2.6**
D and E2 (average)	26.6	23.2	**– 3.4**
Difference (A – D/E2)	1.6	7.6	
excludes canned, processed and frozen			
Total fruit (oz/person/week):*			
A	35.4	53.6	**+ 18.2**
D and E2 (average)	23.6	27.6	**+ 4.0**
Difference (A – D/E2)	11.8	26.0	
includes canned and juice			
Nutrient (amount per person per day):			
Vitamin C (mg):			
A	70	75	**+5**
D and E2 (average)	52	50	**-2**
Difference (A-D/E2)	22	25	
Total vitamin A (ret.equiv) μg			
A	1,350	720	**-630**
D and E2 (average)	1,385	760	**-625**
Difference (A-D/E2)	-35	-40	

- In 1979,
  - income group A was households with income £145+ per week;
  - income group D was households with income below £56 per week;
  - income group E2 was households without an earner with income below £56 per week.

- In 1999,
  - income group A was households with income £655+ per week;
  - income group D was households with income below £165 per week;
  - income group E2 was households without an earner and income below £165 per week.

is regarded as a luxury. The table also shows the differences in intakes of two of the nutrients associated with fresh fruit and vegetables (vitamin C and carotene).

Parents and children in households with little money to spend on food are more likely to eat the same foods as one another, at the same time, whereas those in richer households tend to eat different foods from one another, and to eat at different times from one another – there is more variety in meal types as well as actual foods. Richer people are also more likely to eat the 'own brand' foods from large-chain supermarkets, whereas poorer households tend to eat the commercial brands, partly because these are what are stocked in local shops on deprived estates, and partly because children prefer them and will eat them. The surveys suggest that those who are poor in the UK eat monotonous diets with little variation: they have a much less diverse food base. Everyone has times when they have to 'make do' with what's in the cupboard; being

---

BOX 3.2: **Typical meals for black and white lone parent income support claimants (all names changed)**

One weekday's meals for a white family living on income support

(1992) weekly income of £113.00 and spend about £45.00 each week on food

Family details:	mother (age 40), unemployed, no car
	grandfather (aged 70)
	daughter Becky (aged 12)
	daughter Paula (aged 7)
	All the children had free school meals
	son Alan (aged 11)

BREAKFAST

Mum	Tea (milk & sugar)
Grandfather	Crumpets with Anchor butter, tea
Becky	Crumpets with Anchor butter, tea
Alan	2 slices of toast (Kwik Save, white sliced), with margarine, tea
Paula	Sugar Puffs with milk

LUNCH (12 noon)

Mum (home)	Pink Salmon sandwich (Kwik Save brown bread, Anchor butter, tinned salmon), tea
Grandfather	Same as mum
Becky (school)	Pasty, orange drink, apple crumble & custard

| Paula (school) | Chicken nuggets, beetroot, bubble gum drink, cake & custard |
| Alan (school) | Chicken nuggets, spaghetti, chips and cake |

AFTER SCHOOL (4.15 pm)

Mum, Becky, Paula and Alan — 1 cream slice each and cup of tea

DINNER (5.30 pm)

Family — All had homemade shepherds pie and cup of tea.
Recipe: Kwik Save minced beef, carrots, onion, Oxo cube and potatoes (mashed with margarine)

One weekday's meals for a black family living on income support

---

(1992) weekly income of £125.00 and spend about £48 each week on food

Family details:
mother (aged 52), unemployed, had a car
son Matthew (aged 20), college
daughter Christina (aged 14)
granddaughter Leslie (aged 7)
nephew John (aged 28), college
Leslie had free school meals

BREAKFAST

Mum	Milky coffee (made with milk only) and 2 teaspoons of sugar, 1 slice brown thick sliced toast with mango jam
Matthew	2 slices brown bread toast with mango jam, glass of orange juice
Christina	Same as Matthew
Leslie	Same as Matthew (only 1 slice of toast)
John	1 slice of brown bread toast, cup of tea with milk & sugar

MID-MORNING

| Mum | Cup of coffee with milk & sugar, 1 apple |

LUNCH

Mum	Cheese & tomato sandwich (2 slices brown bread, Tesco margarine) orange squash
Matthew	Meal at college canteen: sausages, chips, gravy, mixed vegetables; rice pudding, 1 apple, glass of water
Christina	Packed lunch prepared by mum: 2 egg sandwiches (margarine, 4 slices brown bread, boiled eggs); 3 digestive biscuits; 1 Mars Bar; 1 small bottle of lemonade
Leslie	School dinner: chicken nuggets, salad and a fruit yoghurt; carton of orange juice (taken from home)
John	Same as mum

```
DINNER (8 PM)
Family                  All had mackerel with vegetable soup and ground rice.
                        Ingredients for the vegetable soup: spinach, plum tomatoes,
                        onions, hot peppers, salt and mixed herbs.
Mum and Christina       I apple each
Leslie                  Banana
```

poor is having to 'make do' from a few basic foods week after week after week, because there is no money left for variety. Box 3.2 shows meals typically eaten by lone parent families studied in 1992/3 in London.

In a study on nutrition and diet in lone parents carried out in 1992/3, a healthy diet score was constructed from a food frequency questionnaire and weighed intake dietary survey.[17] Those who were poorest in material terms had the worst healthy diet scores. Parents who said they tried to prepare meals from a variety of raw ingredients and for whom 'fresh', healthy food was a priority in shopping, had higher healthy diet scores, even when living on income support. Black parents also scored well on the healthy diet indicator, perhaps because in the survey they were the most likely to say they shopped around and cooked from a variety of foodstuffs.

A recent analysis of the *Health Survey for England* used the same healthy diet indicator to investigate the effect on health of material, structural poverty, and social support or 'social capital'. It found that those who lacked material and financial resources were the most likely to eat a poor quality diet. Those who experienced high levels of stress did not have a worse quality diet, although there was a relationship with poor health and, among women, a greater likelihood of smoking. Where people said they received good social support from friends or relatives, they were less likely to smoke and to report a better quality of diet. This was true even when the analysis was adjusted for the strong socio-economic factors which are associated with dietary quality and smoking.[18] These studies were trying to tease out the effects of income, or socioeconomic position, on dietary patterns, from the effects of social support and networks, and confidence to shop and prepare healthier fresh food. They provide some evidence that social and structural factors (being good shops) can make some difference to healthy diet indicators, even where incomes are low.

Studies of adolescents in Scotland have confirmed that dietary patterns similar to those in adults are observed in mid-teens. One study found that adolescents from non-manual and wealthier families, especially if female and non-smokers, were more likely to choose a diet which conformed to healthy eating advice. Another found that, by the age of 15, there was clear differentiation in food choices and meal patterns according to gender, parental social class and own future labour market position.[19]

There have not been many in-depth surveys of patterns of foods eaten by young children, apart from the national survey data shown above. One recent study of three-year olds in the Bristol area found that children were more likely to eat a diet based on convenience foods such as sausages, burgers, chips and other fried foods, pizzas, crisps, sweets, fizzy drinks and take-aways if their mothers were young, less educated, facing severe financial difficulties, and renting council flats. Children whose diets were healthier, who ate more rice, pasta, pulses, vegetables, salads, fish, water and fruit juices, were more likely to have mothers with higher education or who were vegetarians.[20]

This survey was unusual in that it explored in detail how factors such as mother's age, educational attainment or family accommodation actually affect what children eat. The findings suggest that children whose families are poorer are more likely to conform to eating the foods heavily promoted by advertisements. The questions that were not addressed were: do poorer mothers just not have enough money to buy 'healthier' foods; or is it that there are fewer shops selling them near where they live; or are those who have left school with fewer qualifications and are young themselves, less likely to be confident enough to resist what advertisers persuade families they should buy?

NUTRIENT INTAKES

FAMILIES

The *National Food Survey* shows that intakes of many key vitamins and minerals are lower as a proportion of the reference intakes for those with the lowest incomes in the survey, or in households with more than three children, or those headed by a lone parent. The difference between those in the highest income group and the lowest is very noticeable for calcium, iron, magnesium, folate and, particularly, vitamin C. In fact, nutrient intakes among the poorest fifth of families has declined dramatically over the last two decades: vitamin C by 23 per cent and (ß-carotene (vitamin A) by 47 per cent.[21] Consumption of food and energy intakes have fallen over the last 20 years, as people lead more sedentary lives, and diets need to become more nutrient dense to compensate. Richer households have made this adjustment and have more nutrient dense diets than those in the lowest income groups for every nutrient, and the density gap between the rich and poor has widened.[22]

MEN AND WOMEN

The *National Diet and Nutrition Surveys* measure food and nutrient intake by individuals, and although they do not measure household income, they present data by social class based on occupation, receipt of means-tested benefits, household composition or employment status, which can be used as proxy indicators of economic well being. The survey on adults was carried out in the late 1980s (the most recent survey will be published soon) and showed that men and women who were unemployed, or in households claiming benefit, or in social classes IV and V, had significantly lower intakes of iron, fibre, calcium, zinc, vitamin C and vitamin A than people not in these categories. This survey found no differences in fat intakes, or fat as a percentage of total energy, by any social indicator. There are similar findings from other national surveys.

In the survey of lone-parent households (p50) the diets of income support claimants were much less likely to be adequate in terms of reference levels than of those not claiming benefits.[23] These findings were largely independent of smoking habits, and parental attitudes to shopping, cooking and health. The survey also looked at the cumulative effects of living on a low income. Some results are shown in figure 3.2: nutrient intakes were very much less likely to be adequate in the long-term unemployed who live in local authority housing on means-tested benefits, particularly where automatic deductions were made from those benefits for rent or fuel debt recovery. About one in five income support claimants face deductions such as these (over a million households). Those living in the worst deprivation had about half the nutrient intakes of parents not in such circumstances. Their present and future health were likely to be in serious jeopardy.

PREGNANT WOMEN

There have been few large scale surveys of diets and nutrient intakes for women who are pregnant. In studies carried out in the 1980s, diets of pregnant women from low socio-economic groups were found to be

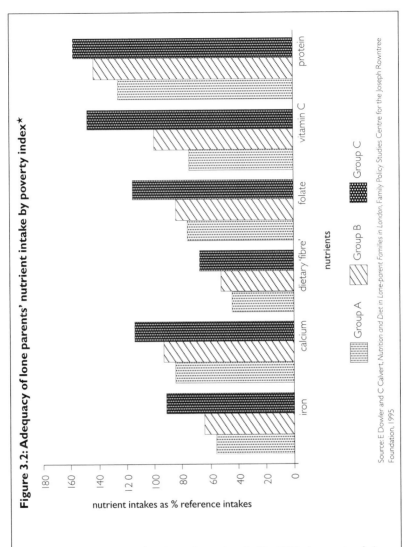

Figure 3.2: Adequacy of lone parents' nutrient intake by poverty index*

Source: E Dowler and C Calvert, *Nutrition and Diet in Lone-parent Families in London*, Family Policy Studies Centre for the Joseph Rowntree Foundation, 1995

Group A = long term unemployed council tenants, no holiday AND whose rent or fuel (and arrears) are automatically deducted from benefit, or paid via a key meter;
Group B = EITHER unemployed council tenants OR with rent/fuel deductions;
Group C = neither category.

The lower a group's mean nutrient intakes are as a percentage of reference intakes the less likely it is that all members of the group are consuming enough of that nutrient to avoid deficiency and maintain health.

far below the reference values for most nutrients, and especially for iron, vitamins A and C, and folic acid (a B vitamin particularly important in the early stages of pregnancy to reduce the risk of neural tube defects such as spina bifida).[24] Again, poorer women were consuming a less varied, less nutrient dense diet than those with adequate incomes. In 1995, the Maternity Alliance and NCH Action for Children combined to survey the food experiences and diets of pregnant women who were living on less than £100 a week. The majority were eating an inadequate diet, and many were missing meals regularly because they could not afford to buy food for themselves, or, if they had them, their other children. The less women were spending on food, the less likely they were to be eating breakfast cereals, fruit or vegetables, or drinking milk and fruit juice. More than two thirds of those studied had iron intakes that were so low as to compromise their health, and nearly two in five had very low intakes of folic acid.[25]

Smoking during pregnancy is known to be bad for the health of the mother and the baby. Smokers are also less likely to eat healthily. Many women try to cut down the number of cigarettes they smoke when pregnant, and some take supplements of iron, folic acid and multi-vitamins. One recent study of pregnant women in Portsmouth measured dietary intakes along with smoking practices, and found that even light smokers had poorer intakes of most vitamins and minerals than non-smokers; only iron and folic acid intakes were improved by supplement use.[26] This study found that the mother's age was an important predictor of the quality of her diet. Younger women had worse diets than older women of similar social class and education levels, especially if they smoked (which they were more likely to do). For instance, intakes of vitamin C and ß-carotene (a form of vitamin A found mainly in vegetables) in smokers under 24 years were almost half the levels of non-smokers aged 28 and over.

Another study of pregnant women in the Avon area found that those who said they had the greatest difficulty affording food, clothing, heating, housing and things for the baby, had the worst diets – again, vitamin C, folic acid, iron, zinc and ß-carotene were very low, particularly among smokers.[27] Those who had least money were more likely than any others to eat chips, sausages, pies and pasties, and less likely to eat green vegetables, salad and fruit or fruit juice. The foods they chose were good to counter hunger, but they were high in saturated fats with low levels of vitamins and minerals.

Birthweight is an important indicator of the infant's likely wellbeing in the future. The Avon study found no evidence that mothers who said they could not afford to buy food subsequently had babies of lower birthweights, unless they smoked. As is usually the case in such studies, smoking and parity were the strongest predictors of low birthweight. This finding should not be taken to mean mothers are simply responsible for their babies' low birth weight because they had continued to smoke during pregnancy. As Spencer argues in his powerful book on *Poverty and Child Health*:[28]

> Birthweight is the end result of a complex process influenced by the woman's own diet and experience in childhood, and her present and past social support and level of stress. Smoking cannot be disentangled from this complex of cumulative influences in which the main determinant is social structure [...]

The Avon study was unusual in that, instead of using the usual research indicators of socio-economic status, such as education, occupation or housing tenure, the mothers' own sense of their financial wellbeing was used. The researchers found that asking mothers about whether they could afford things was a good guide to the quality of their diets. In the study of lone-parent families they were also asked whether they could afford as much fresh food as they wanted for themselves or their children. Again, answers to this straightforward question, where the parent themselves decided what they meant by 'afford', 'fresh food', 'enough', produced a very good indicator of poverty and hardship. Those who answered 'no' had worse dietary patterns, and lower nutrient intakes, than those who said 'yes' or 'sometimes'. This might seem obvious: people know what their own circumstances are. Yet usually in social, health or nutritional surveys, researchers do not rely on subjective indicators of socio-economic status – people's own views. They usually use measures that are said to be more objective and less specifically to do with money, such as occupation or housing.

BABIES, INFANTS AND YOUNG CHILDREN UNDER FIVE

Breastfeeding is fundamental both for the baby's immediate wellbeing and for long term health. Infants grow very rapidly after birth, and breast milk supplies all the nutrients and energy needed, in the right balance, to enable healthy growth. It also contains immunoglobulins, antimicrobial agents, and other protective factors against infection. Breastfeeding avoids early exposure to inappropriate dietary antigens (such as from cow's milk or gluten), and it lowers the risk of infections and of atopic diseases such as asthma. It probably also promotes brain and cognitive development. Breastfeeding may contribute to limiting the development of childhood obesity and of non-insulin dependent diabetes in later life, although the evidence for these benefits is more controversial. Mothers gain too: their psychosocial interactions with their child improve, they are more likely to get back to normal weight after pregnancy, and in the longer term lower their risk of pre-menopausal breast cancer.

Several surveys have shown that breastfeeding rates in the lowest socio-economic groups are about half those of the highest (44 per cent choosing to initiate breastfeeding compared to 81 per cent).[29] Mothers are recommended to breastfeed for at least four to six months, but although on average in the UK about two thirds of mothers breastfeed at birth, this drops to one in five, only partially breastfeeding, by six months. This is one of the lowest rates in Europe (in Northern Ireland only 8 per cent; in Sweden it is 73 per cent of mothers). Poorer educated, single and younger mothers are least likely to initiate breastfeeding, and those who do, stop sooner. Several surveys have shown that infants from the lowest socio-economic groups are more likely to be anaemic, partly because they are more likely to be premature, with low iron stores, and to be fed cow's milk from a very early age. They are also more likely to experience common infections as a result.

The national and smaller scale nutrition surveys show that young children who come from manual social classes, or households claiming benefits, or from loneparent families, have much lower intakes and blood levels of most vitamins and minerals than those not in these circumstances. When the measurements are adjusted to take account of differences in the amount of total food eaten, even then, children from manual homes have proportionally lower amounts of ß-carotene, niacin, vitamins B12, C and E, and higher intakes of starch. This suggests these children were not eating less food, they were eating different food. In fact, there were no differences in energy intake by any socio-economic characteristic. The national surveys also looked at the body stores of vitamins and iron by measuring blood levels; these too were lower in children from manual homes, or where the head of household was unemployed, claimed means-tested benefits, or was a lone-parent. There is some evidence that lower intakes of antioxidants and zinc may be associated with a higher risk of asthma.[30]

Low iron status and iron-deficiency anaemia are significant problems in Britain among children under five years in general, and worse among low income families and among Asian children. In a general practice survey in Bristol, 16 per cent of children under 5 years were iron deficient and nearly 6 per cent were actually anaemic. The Afro-Caribbean children were even more likely to be iron deficient (24 per cent).[31] An intervention programme for children living in multiple deprivation in Birmingham found that a third of the children aged 18-24 months had haemoglobin levels below reference levels. Few of the children had been breastfed beyond three months, and, as in other surveys, many had had cow's milk and diets with few iron-rich foods for much of their lives.[32] Vitamin C improves the absorption of iron from vegetable sources, while foods such as tea or eggs inhibit absorption of non-haem (ie, non-meat) iron in the diet. Unfortunately, many low income children regularly eat diets low in vitamin C, so they do not absorb what little iron is in their food, very well.

SCHOOL-AGED CHILDREN

Many people – parents, teachers, school governors, health professionals – often worry about school children's diets. The recent report of the national survey shows that many young people still eat more sugar, salt and saturated fat than is good for them, and not enough fruit and vegetables. Only a fifth of girls aged 15 –18 eat citrus fruit, but on average girls drank 1.5 litres of fizzy drinks in a week. Boys of the same age drank even more fizzy drinks (>2 litres) and ate 500g of chips in a week: equivalent to a portion every weekday. Even children aged 7–10 years ate 300g chips in a week. Younger boys and girls ate, by weight, nearly four times as many biscuits or sweets as green vegetables. Far too few take adequate exercise or enjoy any physical activity, although there are not usually large socio-economic differences in school based physical activity.

Most nutrient intakes were worse in young people in households of lower socio-economic status, whether measured by receipt of benefit, household income or social class. Children from poorer households had lower intakes of energy, fat, most vitamins and minerals. In both boys and girls, intakes of vitamin C, calcium, phosphorus, magnesium and iodine, pantothenic acid for boys and riboflavin, niacin, ß-carotene and manganese for girls remained lower when differences in energy intakes were taken into account: again children were eating different food or lower nutritional quality, not just less food. Those in lower socio-economic groups also tended to have lower blood or urine levels of folate, riboflavin, vitamins C, D and iron. These biochemical measurements confirm that their body stores of nutrients were low, or that the differences seen were not just artefacts of measuring dietary intakes.

The *Health Survey for England* in 1997 included food measurements (by a food frequency questionnaire) on 14,500 children aged 2-15 years. Only a fifth of the sample said they ate fruit or vegetables more than once a day, but the proportion of boys and girls who said they did decreased markedly from social classes I and II (combined) to classes IV and V (combined) and from the highest to the lowest income quintile. The proportion who said they consumed sweet foods, chips, crisps and to a lesser extent, soft drinks, more than once a day also decreased from social classes I and II to IV and V, and from the highest to the lowest income quintiles.

Lower iron status in children is likely to inhibit physical activity levels and is associated with lower bone mineral density (and therefore lower peak bone mass in adulthood, which has consequences for subsequent osteoporosis).[33] If adolescents with lower iron status become pregnant, they are more likely to experience a stillbirth, or produce a low birth weight baby.[34]

POOR FAMILIES' HEALTH

There is more and more research on inequalities in health and wellbeing both in Britain and in other developed countries. There are measurable differences in health profiles and the likelihood of dying earlier than might be expected between socio-economic groups, defined in various ways. Much research now looks at the processes by which such inequalities are created and maintained.[35]

THE IMPACT OF BABIES' EXPERIENCES IN THE WOMB ON SUBSEQUENT HEALTH

Mothers' nutrient intakes are important for their own and their babies' wellbeing. But the relationship between maternal nutritional status and measurable outcomes such as birthweight are not easily understood. Women throughout the world have managed to produce reasonably healthy babies on food intakes throughout pregnancy that are very low in essential nutrients. There has been a lot of research on what causes babies to have low birthweight, more commonly found in poorer parts of the world, and on strategies to improve their wellbeing.[36] In the last decade or so, much new evidence has accumulated about the impact of under-nutrition that the foetus experiences while still in the womb, and long-term health outcomes (see Box 3.3 on foetal origins hypothesis). Babies who are thinner or shorter at birth than would be expected – which is a sign they have experienced nutritional problems in the womb – have been shown to be at greater risk of developing, respectively, non-insulin dependent diabetes, or coronary heart disease, as adults, especially if they grow poorly in the first year of life and subsequently become obese as adults.[37] They are also at increased risk of raised blood pressure and stroke. It is important to realise this evidence is not about babies defined as low birthweight (<2500g at birth): these are babies born within the normal range of weights, but who are either thin (low ponderal index: birthweight/length) or short (low length/ gestational age) at birth.

What is less clear is what nutritional interventions are needed, and at what stage, to make a difference. Current thinking is that improving the nutritional status of teenage girls, well before their first pregnancy, might

---

BOX 3.3: **Foetal origins hypothesis**

There has been accumulating evidence that malnutrition at certain, critical phases of development before, and soon after, birth causes permanent change to structures and metabolic processes. This 'biological programming' is in turn said to lead to impaired function or health, or can predispose the individual to the risk of impaired function if an additional insult is added in later life. For instance, adults who were smaller than expected at birth, which is a sign of foetal malnutrition, are at high risk of non-insulin dependent diabetes and impaired glucose tolerance if they become obese in adult life.[38]

There is still some controversy about the hypothesis and its determinist slant, although experimental evidence from animal studies, and longitudinal epidemiological evidence from data sets spanning many decades, increasingly support it. Events and processes that affect the foetus while developing in the womb can be directly related to adult physiology and disease risk. However, social and biological factors in the adult's life interact with this very early nutritional experience to increase susceptibility to ill-health.

Both the foetal environment and adult risk factors are strongly socially determined. A mother's health during pregnancy depends on her health and experience throughout her life, and the full foetal development depends on good placental function, low infection, plenty of exercise, not smoking or drinking alcohol and an adequate diet during pregnancy. All these depend on her family and social circumstances.

have the most effect. But certainly, all mothers' nutritional status is likely to be important in ensuring the foetus' nutritional conditions are good.

LIFE COURSE ANALYSIS OF HEALTH INEQUALITIES

> A woman in a low-income household is more likely to be poorly nour-
> ished during pregnancy and to produce a low birth weight or premature
> baby. A child growing up in a low-income household is more likely to
> be disadvantaged in terms of diet, crowding, safe areas in which to play
> and opportunities for educational achievement. An adolescent from a
> low-income household is more likely to leave education at the mini-
> mum school leaving age, with few qualifications and to experience
> unemployment before entering a low-paid insecure and hazardous
> occupation, with no occupational pension scheme. An adult working in
> this sector of the labour market is more likely to experience periods of
> unemployment, to raise a family in financially difficult circumstances
> and to retire early [....] A retired person who does not have an occupa-
> tional pension is more likely to experience financial deprivation in the
> years leading up to their death.[39]

There is much interest and research now on the clustering of advantage or disadvantage over the course of a person's life, and how that mediates poor health and early death. That those who are poorer in material terms get sick more often, and die younger, is well documented and has been the subject of government committees and research pro-grammes.[40] The differentials between mortality among the richest and poorest widened in Britain as income inequality and deprivation increased during the 1970s and 1980s. That is, as individuals have become poorer, and as British society became more unequal, the risk of illness and early death for those who are poor has increased relative to those who are not poor. What is becoming clearer is that cross sectional studies, which relate present outcome indicators such as sickness, or even mortality, to current socio-economic status of adults, do not offer the best account of what is happening. Instead, as the Department of Health report in 1995, *Variations in Health*, concluded, we need a life-course perspective on inequalities, that enables us to understand the cumulative effect of differential exposure to health-damaging or health-promoting physical and social environments.[41] For instance, adult height is a good predictor of coronary heart disease, respiratory diseases and some cancers. Much of this association seems to be accounted for by

---

BOX 3.4: Deprivation and obesity

- Adults and children in Britain are more likely to be overweight or obese now than they were in the past.
- Those who are overweight or obese are more at risk of poor health (from coronary heart disease, some cancers, high blood pressure, adult onset diabetes, gallstones, arthritis) and of dying younger.
- The adults who are most likely to be overweight or obese, especially women, are in the lowest socio-economic classes, or unemployed, or claiming benefits.
- This pattern is now being seen in children: poorer children are more likely to be overweight or obese, especially older girls.
- Parents who are overweight are more likely be living with children who are overweight; you are also more likely to be overweight or obese as an adult if you are overweight as a child (although rates of obesity generally are going up generally).
- It is difficult to disentangle the key factors in childhood which contribute to being overweight or obese, but:
  - there is no clear relationship between the method of infant feeding and subsequent obesity;
  - there is some evidence that children who grow poorly in their early life, and then eat a calorie dense diet, are more likely to become overweight or obese;
  - physical activity is very important as well as diet;
  - whether children (and adults) experience psychological or emotional deprivation is probably also important, as are cultural norms and expectations.

Sources: Health Development Agency, *Coronary Heart Disease: Guidelines for implementing preventive aspects of the National Health Service Framework*, NHS, 2000; Kinra et al, *Journal of Epidemiology and Community Health* 54, 2000, pp456-60

---

lung function, which itself is partly determined by foetal development as well as exposure to childhood chest illnesses and smoking.[42]

IMPACT OF CHILDREN'S FOOD AND NUTRITION ON THEIR INTELLECTUAL DEVELOPMENT

Nutrition in early life has a big impact on development of the brain; diet in certain critical periods seems to be crucial for health and performance later on. A recent long term study by the Medical Research Council showed that pre-term babies given 'standard' instead of 'enriched' infant formula had a much lower overall IQ and lower verbal IQ at eight years old. This effect was particularly seen in the boys (47 per cent given standard formula compared to 13 per cent given enriched, had verbal IQ levels <85).[43] Low birthweight is itself associated with reduced cognitive function, not only in childhood, but even on into adulthood.[44] Babies from poorer families are more likely to be given standard infant formula, even if pre-term, and are more likely to be low birth weight.

Dietary deficiency and poor nutritional status in children, even in milder forms, can have detrimental effects on cognitive development, behaviour, concentration and school performance. These things are difficult to measure consistently, and it is also difficult to separate out the direct effects of children's diets from the social and cultural aspects of their environment. Nonetheless, there is much evidence that children who come to school hungry or tired, or generally undernourished, cannot learn properly or benefit from teaching. They are also more likely to play truant. Children who have not had breakfast are more likely to suffer short term hunger at school, show impaired memory and attention span, and reduced efficiency of learning (information processing).[45] Children who are hungry are less likely to behave well, or to be able to concentrate properly on what they are doing (to remain 'on task').[46] Children with iron deficiency anaemia are likely to have impaired cognitive function, and may have lower IQ.[47]

SUMMARY

- National and local surveys of food and dietary intake can be used to look at the adequacy of diets for health, for adults, young people, children and infants.
- All surveys show that there is less variety in dietary patterns, and more monotony of foodstuffs, in poorer households.
- People in poorer households are less likely to eat fresh fruit, wholemeal bread, lean meat, oily fish – all of which are recommended for healthy living.
- At all ages, people in poorer households have lower nutrient intakes than people in richer households, and the gap between them has widened over the last 20 years.
- Pregnant women who live on low incomes have very poor diets indeed; they are more likely to bear low birthweight babies and are less likely to breastfeed their infants.
- Children who are poorly nourished are unlikely to grow well; they are more likely to become obese; children who come to school without breakfast and are hungry are less likely to benefit from schooling and learn well.

NOTES

1 P S Shetty and W P T James, 'Determinants of disease: nutrition', from *The Oxford Textbook of Public Health*, 3rd edition, R Detels, W Holland, J McEwan and S Omenn (eds), Oxford University Press, 1997

2 W P T James, M Nelson, A Ralph and S Leather 'Socioeconomic determinants of health: the contribution of nutrition to inequalities in health', *British Medical Journal*, 314, 1997, pp1545-9

3 Editorial, 'The fetal origins of adult disease', *British Medical Journal*, 322, 2001

4 See note 2; P Shetty and K McPherson (eds) *Diet, Nutrition and Chronic Disease: lessons from contrasting worlds*, John Wiley & Sons, 1997

5 A Marsh and S McKay, *Poor Smokers*, Policy Studies Institute, 1994

6 See note 2

7 Department of Health, *Dietary Reference Values for Food Energy and Nutrients for the United Kingdom*, Report on Health and Social Subjects no 41, HMSO, 1991; this committee has been replaced by The Scientific Advisory Committee on Nutrition (SANC)

8 C Williams, 'Clarifying healthy eating advice', *British Medical Journal*, 310, 1995, pp1453-5; Health Education Authority, *The Balance of Good Health Information Pack*, Health Education Authority, 1996

9 J Boyd Orr, *Food Health and Income: report on a survey of adequacy of diet in relation to income*, Macmillan & Co, 1936; E Dowler and S Leather, 'Spare some change for a bite to eat? from primary poverty to social exclusion: the role of nutrition and food', in: J Bradshaw and R Sainsbury (eds), *Experiencing Poverty*, Ashgate, 2000

10 See for example, G Craig and E Dowler, '"Let them eat cake!" Poverty, hunger and the UK state', in: G Riches (ed), *First World Hunger: Food Security and Welfare Politics*, Macmillan Press, 1997; Department of Health, *Low Income, Food, Nutrition and Health: Strategies for Improvement*. A Report from the Low Income Project Team to the Nutrition Task Force, Department of Health, 1996; S Leather, *The making of modern malnutrition: an overview of food poverty in the UK*, The Caroline Walker Trust, 1996

11 Ministry of Agriculture, Fisheries and Food, *National Food Survey 1999. Annual Report on Food Expenditure, Consumption and Nutrient Intakes*, The Stationery Office, 2000 and earlier. The National Food Survey: is merging with the Family Expenditure Survey in 2002.

12 J Gregory, K Foster, H Tyler and M Wiseman, *The Dietary and Nutritional Survey of British Adults*, HMSO, 1990; J R Gregory, D L Collins, P S W Davies, J M Hughes and P Clarke, *National Diet and Nutrition Survey: children aged 1.5 to 4.5 years*, HMSO, 1995; S Finch, *National diet and nutrition survey people aged 65 years and over: Vol. 1 Report of the diet and nutrition survey*, The Stationery Office, 1998; J R Gregory, *National Diet and Nutrition Survey: young people aged 4-18 years Vol. 1 Report of the diet and nutrition survey*, The Stationery Office, 2000

13 For example: C Bolton-Smith, W C S Smith, M Woodward and H Tunstall-Pedoe, 'Nutrient intakes in different social class groups: results from the Scottish Heart Health Study', *British Journal of Nutrition*, 65, 1991, pp321-325; F E M Braddon, M E J Wadsworth, J M C Davies and H A Cripps, 'Social and regional differences in food and alcohol consumption and their measurement in a national birth cohort', *Journal of Epidemiology and Community Health*, 42, 1988, pp341-349; M E Barker, S I McClean, P G McKenna, N G Reid, J J Strain, K A Thomson, A P Williamson and M E Wright, *Diet, Lifestyle and Health in Northern Ireland. A Report to the Health Promotion Research Trust*, University of Ulster, 1989; M J Whichelow, S W Erzinclioglu and B D Cox, 'Some regional variations in dietary patterns in a random sample of British adults', *European Journal of Clinical Nutrition*, 45, 1991, pp253-262; P Prescott-Clarke and P Primatesta, *Health Survey for England: The Health of Young People 1995-97*, The Stationery Office, 1998

14 For example: S J Darke, M M Disselduff and G P Try, 'A nutrition survey of children from one-parent families in Newcastle-upon-Tyne in 1970', *British Journal of Nutrition*, 44, 1980, pp237-241; W Doyle, M A Crawford, B M Laurance and P Drury, 'Dietary survey during pregnancy in a low socio-economic group', *Human Nutrition: Applied Nutrition*, 36A, 1982, pp95-106; A S Anderson and K Hunt, 'Who are the 'healthy eaters'? Eating patterns and health promotion in the west of Scotland', *Health Education Journal*, 51, 1, 1991, pp3-10

15 M Nelson, 'Childhood nutrition and poverty', *Proceedings of the Nutrition Society*, 59, 2000, pp307-315

16 See note 15

17 E Dowler and C Calvert, *Nutrition and Diet in Lone-parent Families in London*, Family Policy Studies Centre for the Joseph Rowntree Foundation, 1995

18 H Cooper, S Arber, L Fee and J Ginn, *The influence of social support and social capital on health*, Health Education Authority, 1999

19 A S Anderson, S Macintyre and P West, 'Dietary patterns among adolescents in the west of Scotland', *British Journal of Nutrition*, 71(1), 1994, pp111-22; H Sweeting, A S Anderson and P West, 'Socio-demographic correlates of dietary habits in mid to late adolescence', *European Journal of Clinical Nutrition*, 48(10), 1994, pp736-48

20 K North, P Emmett and Avon Longitudinal Study of Pregnancy and Childhood, 'Multivariate analysis of diet among three-year old children and associations with socio-demographic characteristics', *European Journal of Clinical Nutrition*, 54, 200, pp73-80

21 S Leather, *The making of modern malnutrition: an overview of food poverty in the UK*, The Caroline Walker Trust, 1996

22 See note 2

23 See note 17

24 W Doyle, M A Crawford, B M Laurance and P Drury, 'Dietary survey during pregnancy in a low socio-economic group', *Human Nutrition:*

Applied Nutrition 36A, 1982, pp95-106; C Schofield, J Stewart and E Wheeler, 'The diets of pregnant and post-pregnant women in different social groups in London and Edinburgh: calcium, iron, retinol, ascorbic acid and folic acid', *British Journal of Nutrition* 62, 1989, pp363-377

25 J Dallison and T Lobstein, *Poor Expectations: Poverty and undernourishment in pregnancy*, NCH Action for Children and the Maternity Alliance, 1995

26 F Matthews, P Yudkin, R S Smith, A Neil, 'Nutrient intakes during pregnancy: the influence of smoking status and age', *Journal of Epidemiology and Community Health*, 54, 2000, pp17-23

27 I Rogers, P Emmett, D Baker, J Golding and the ASLPAC Study Team, *European Journal of Clinical Nutrition*, 52, 1998, pp251-260

28 N Spencer, *Poverty and Child Health*, Radcliffe Medical Press, 1996, p175

29 British Medical Association, *Growing Up in Britain: Ensuring a healthy future for our children. A study of 0-5 year olds*, BMJ Books, 1999; M Nelson, 'Childhood nutrition and poverty', *Proceedings of the Nutrition Society*, 59, 2000, pp307-315

30 See note 15

31 See note 29

32 See note 29

33 M Nelson, F Bakaliou and A Trivedi 'Iron deficiency anaemia and physical performance in adolescent girls from different ethnic backgrounds', *British Journal of Nutrition*, 72, 1994, pp427-433

34 See note 15

35 R Illsley and P G Svensson, 'Health inequities in Europe', special issue of *Social Science and Medicine*, 31(3), 1990; M Marmot and R G Wilkinson (eds), *Social Determinants of Health*, Oxford University Press, 1999; J Lynch, G Davey Smith, M Hillmeier, M Shaw, T Raghunathan and G Kaplan, 'Income inequality, the psychosocial environment, and health: comparison of wealthy nations', *The Lancet*, 358, 2001, pp194-200

36 A Ashworth, 'Effects of intrauterine growth retardation on mortality and morbidity in infants and young children', *European Journal of Clinical Nutrition*, 52, S1, S34-42, 1997

37 D J P Barker, 'Prenatal influences on disease in later life' and D Leon, 'Discussion' Chapter 2 in: P Shetty and K McPherson (eds), *Diet, Nutrition and Chronic Disease: lessons from contrasting worlds*, John Wiley & Sons, 1997; M Wadsworth, 'Early Life', Chapter 3 in: M Marmot, and R G Wilkinson (eds), *Social Determinants of Health*, Oxford University Press, 1999; British Medical Association, 'Fetal origins of adult disease', Chapter 8 in: *Growing Up in Britain: Ensuring a healthy future for our children. A study of 0-5 year olds*, BMJ Books, 1999

38 See note 37

39 G Davey Smith, D Blane and M Bartley, 'Explanations for socio-economic differentials in mortality: evidence from Britain and elsewhere', *European Journal of Public Health*, 4, 1994, pp131-144

40 D Acheson, *Report of an Independent Inquiry into Inequalities in Health*, Department of Health, 1998; UK Economic and Social Research Council: Research Programme on Health Variations, 1995-ongoing

41 G Davey Smith and E Brunner, 'Socio-economic differentials in health: the role of nutrition', *Proceedings of the Nutrition Society* 56, 1997, pp75-90; N G Norgan, 2000, 'Long-term physiological and economic consequences of growth retardation in children and adolescents', *Proceedings of the Nutrition Society*, 59, 2, 2000, pp245-256

42 G Davey Smith et al, 'Height and risk of death among men and women: aetiological implications of associations with cardiorespiratory disease and cancer mortality', *Journal of Epidemiology and Community Health*, 54, 2000, pp97-103

43 A Lucas, R Morley and T J Cole, 'Randomised trial of early diet in preterm babies and later intelligence quotient', *British Medical Journal*, 317, 1998, pp1481-7

44 H T Sørensen, S Sabroe, J Olsen, K J Rothman, M W Gillman and P Fischer, 'Birth weight and cognitive function in young adult life: historical cohort study', *British Medical Journal*, 315, 1997, pp401-403

45 D T Simeon and S Grantham-McGregor, 'Effect of missing breakfast on the cognitive functions of school children of different nutritional status', *American Journal of Clinical Nutrition*, 49, 1989, pp646-653

46 C Ani and S Grantham-McGregor, 'The effects of breakfast on educational performance, attendance and classroom behaviour', in: N Donovan and C Street (eds), *Fit for School: how breakfast clubs meet health, education and childcare needs*, New Policy Institute, 1999

47 See note 15

4 MANAGING TO EAT ON A LOW INCOME

There have been many studies, at national level and on smaller samples, which examine what life is like for those defined as poor, or who see themselves as poor. However, as Elaine Kempson has pointed out:

> There is no clear point at which people can be said to live in poverty; it is a matter of degree. The poorer people are, the more difficult it becomes to make ends meet, with the very poorest finding it difficult to cover even the necessities, such as food, heating and a roof over their heads. [...] On a lower income, people try to cut back spending on essentials; while those on the very lowest incomes face either going without food or fuel or getting into debt. As a consequence the struggle to make ends meet not only affects family life, but can result in poor diet, lack of fuel and water, poor housing and homelessness, debt, poor physical health and stress and mental health problems.[1]

CUTTING BACK ON FOOD EXPENDITURE

In study after study, people interviewed say similar things in relation to managing a tight budget. Although not everyone puts a specific amount aside each week or month to pay for food, as they might for rent or household bills, people can nonetheless say almost exactly what they spend on food, and where. Food is seen as one of the most important items of expenditure (many try to rank it first, above rent), and therefore something bought first on the day people receive their state benefits or wages. People often say they do this to control their spending, by buying essentials during one main shopping trip; it is also the case that a rapid main shop is usually necessary because most essentials are running out by the time they receive their money. Some people do talk of ways of spreading food expenditure over the week, or longer periods (for instance, they might cash their child benefit at the end of the week to be able to buy food for the weekend), but such strategies are usually contingent on parent(s) having extra sources of support, whether from occasional or regular wages, an absent parent in the case of a lone parent, or from friends or their family.

Many say they consciously try not to cut back on food, but sometimes have to in order to pay a pressing bill, although cigarettes (among smokers), clothing and shoes are usually mentioned first as being things to cut back on if you need money. There is no doubt that food expenditure is the most flexible item on the 'essentials' budget list. However, in several studies, when asked about cutting back, people said that they already spent so little on food they did not feel they could cut back further. Most people said they bought very little fruit, and ate less meat or fish than they would like.

> I buy apples and bananas every fortnight [...] It's horrible when she has a banana and then says, 'Can I have an apple?' and you've got to stop her because it's got to last.

> [when money for food is running out...] I improvise. One week I had only milk and flour so I made milk buns; they really filled us up![2]

People adopt a variety of strategies for managing money, which probably reflect underlying attitudes to paying bills or meeting costs of living, although it is likely people cannot always put their ideals into practice because of external circumstances as well as age and experience.[3] Many budget by buying stamps to pay for future bills, or have rent or fuel deducted automatically from benefits, or use fuel key meters, as strategies to prevent gas or electricity being cut off (not always strategies of choice). However, many keys users in fact pay a higher rate than regular users because they are paying back arrears, as are those whose fuel costs are deducted from benefits. People in these circumstances often describe themselves as 'robbing Peter to pay Paul': making ends meet is a constant struggle, and families often run out of money for food. They also have much lower nutrient intakes than households who do not use these strategies (see Figure 3.2).

> One family had been living on benefit for over eight years and budgeted extremely rigidly. They set aside a fixed sum for bills and savings each week and the remainder they spent on food. If the bills were higher than

expected they spent less on food, rather than draw upon savings. For example, one week the family could not afford to eat anything other than beans on toast because an electricity bill was higher than they had expected.[4]

WHERE AND HOW PEOPLE SHOP FOR FOOD

I buy vegetables, they are valuable for nutrition and rice for energy. I don't buy fruit routinely if money is not enough […] I go [to the market] around 10 o'clock on Saturday. I find they have slashed their prices remarkably. […] If you're a mother you get to know where to go to save a few coins.[5]

Kwik Save is just your basic. Asda and Sainsbury's are better. But it's depressing, you go into Sainsbury's or somewhere like that and everyone's nicely dressed. You don't find poor people in Sainsbury's and you see those other places and you say, where do I belong? I feel like I don't belong in the really poor one and I don't belong in the really rich one.[6]

People say they keep their regular food expenditure low by shopping in markets or discount stores, or by relying heavily on 'bargains' or 'money-off' offers in supermarkets. These strategies take a lot of time even for basic food shopping, hunting for bargains and knowing where to go, when. Food shopping is never the relatively relaxed and enjoyable affair as is described by those with more disposable income. Families make good use of a freezer, if they have one, or even bulk buy with friends, or use the community based food co-ops springing up. However, those with limited weekly income often find bulk-buying difficult, either because they and their friends cannot accumulate sufficient cash, or because purchasing 'little and often' has to be a deliberate ploy to restrict family members' casual consumption of what has been purchased for specific meals. Some families simply cannot plan sufficiently ahead to place orders with a food co-op, not knowing whether they will have the money to pay for a week's vegetables and fruit in one go.

You're more tired. I mean just the thing that being poor is so much work, your whole life. You see people going into a shop, they buy what they want and they leave. But you're there, you're having to calculate how much money you've got as you go round, you're having to look at one brand then another, and meanwhile the store detective is looking over your shoulder which is also work having to cope with that kind of scrutiny, because you are poor they expect you to take something.[7]

In fact, shopping for food is often a miserable experience for those on low incomes: many find it depressing, frustrating and demoralising because of the lack of choice. Despite an often expressed desire to look for food that is fresh and healthy, or value-for-money, parents say that, of necessity, price is what governs which food they buy and how much. People talk of 'counting pennies' whenever they go to the shops, and of constantly juggling money to make ends meet. People who live in these circumstances do not use the terms 'coping/budgeting strategy' to describe what they do: they incorporate this behaviour into every-day life. Indeed, long term benefit recipients, and families in work on low wages, take these adaptations for granted:

> I'm so used to not having any money, it's just how we live.

> You get used to watching what you spend and thinking to yourself, can I buy that cheaper from somewhere else, it gets to the point when you don't realize that you're doing it any more.

> You know, I work all the hours I can so that we can manage a bit better but it doesn't seem to make a difference, the money goes and you're back to counting pennies.[8]

Several studies have found that the less money families have to spend on food the more often they go shopping: they buy food on a daily basis. This is mainly because parents have found that if there is food in the house it gets eaten, which often leaves none for the following day. Another strategy mothers with little money adopt is to shop alone. If partners or older children accompany them they say they spend more money, and there are arguments about what should be bought.

EATING PATTERNS

People living on low incomes cook and prepare food as cheaply as possible. Mothers in particular often eat sandwiches or crackers, which need no cooking. Parents and children usually eat the same foods as one another, at the same time, unlike the majority of the British population, where household members eat different things from one another, at different times.

> We'd sit down and eat in the evenings together but sometimes I get fed up of eating with the kids and I'd love to have my dinner just with [her husband] later in the evening but the kids can't wait. They're hungry when they come in from school and it's all I can get them to do to wait until tea time.

> We always eat with the children and have done for a long time but it'd be nice not having to.[9]

Families on low incomes typically buy the same foods and eat the same meals all the time, with little variation, partly because of economies of scale, and partly because they have little opportunity for experimenting with new foods. Parents nearly always say they have to buy food they know their children will eat; they cannot afford to try new dishes, or have food rejected or thrown away, when they would have to offer an alternative – which they cannot afford to stock. The other side of this coin is that parents, particularly mothers, will do anything they can to protect their children from the effects of poverty, and often go without. The survey on lone parents found that those with school aged children often seem to eat very little themselves during the day. In the *Small Fortunes* research on the lifestyles and living standards of British children nearly a fifth of mothers regularly went without food to enable their children to eat, particularly if they were lone parents on income support.[10] Few parents admit to letting their children go hungry.

> I always have something in for real emergencies! I would never get that bad.

> If we're really stuck we can go to my mum's.[11]

We have pointed out in Chapter 2 that many studies have shown low income households often rely on 'convenience' foods (burgers, sausages, pies, pizzas, fish fingers). People often have clear ideas about what constitutes a 'proper meal' (meat and two vegetables; something eaten at a table), and say that, although they cannot afford it all the time, they try to have a family meal once or twice a week. Many say they 'eat a roast dinner' on Sunday, but what they often mean is in fact a very simple, cheap meal – not the traditional 'roast with trimmings' that people actually want to be able to provide.

> We try to eat 'proper' meals like meat and veg and that, but there isn't the money to do it all the time. So we eat properly once or twice a week, depending on the money, and the rest of the time we make do with

things like sausages, pies, potatoes and things like [baked] beans. The meals aren't as good but they do the job, they'll fill them up and stop them from being hungry. It's the best I can do.[12]

In fact, most parents and their children describe their diets as dull and monotonous, especially when money is running out because a large bill has to be paid, or the day before their benefit it due. People talk of eating 'pot luck stew or pasta', made with whatever can be found in the cupboard or freezer (if they have one), or rice with a bit of sauce, or even just toast. Mothers become 'canny' at dealing with children's demands. For instance, many children will only eat branded foods such as Kellogg's cornflakes, or drink branded drinks such as Coca Cola. Mothers make one purchase of the branded good and then refill the empty packaging or bottle with cheaper unbranded alternatives. Some even hide foods, such as biscuits and treats, to make sure they last.

Families manage to feed themselves and no one else. Those who cannot afford to invite other family members and friends to eat with them are often reluctant to accept invitations to eat outside the home. Families with children try hard to continue to invite their children's friends round again because they do not want them to be excluded. But this always involves careful planning to buy things such as pizza, chips and drinks. This is partly because, as noted in Chapter 1, the children only wanted to eat brand named foods which were more expensive.[13]

There are 'technically homeless' households with dependent children, often headed by lone parents, who are housed by local authorities in 'bed and breakfast' accommodation. Many of these families have problems storing and preparing food: they often have nowhere, or nowhere satisfactory, to cook, and have to rely on takeaway foods and sandwiches.

SUMMARY

- People adopt many careful strategies to manage to put food on the table.
- Some strategies for managing a limited budget (such as catalogue payment, or key meters) have severe consequences for dietary quality because they use up ready cash, so people have to rely on a few, very limited, basic foodstuffs.
- Parents go without food, or without tasty elements of the meal, to enable their children to have the best of what is available.

- People struggle to invite friends or family for food to socialise or even celebrate events like children's birthdays.
- Those who live in 'bed and breakfast' accommodation face severe problems in storing, preparing and eating food.

NOTES

1 E Kempson, *Life on a Low Income*, YPS for the Joseph Rowntree Foundation, 1996

2 Lone parent on income support, quoted in E Dowler and C Calvert, *Nutrition and Diet in Lone-parent Families in London*, Family Policy Studies Centre for the Joseph Rowntree Foundation, 1995, pp36 and 38.

3 E Kempson, A Bryson and K Rowlingson, *Hard Times: How poor families make ends meet*, Policy Studies Institute, 1994; E Dowler, 'Budgeting for food on a low income: the case of lone parents', *Food Policy*, 22, 5, 1998, pp405-17

4 B Dobson, A Beardsworth, T Keil and R Walker, *Diet, Choice and Poverty: Social, cultural and nutritional aspects of food consumption among low income families*, Family Policy Studies Centre with the Joseph Rowntree Foundation, 1994, p51

5 Lone mother, a middle-aged nurse with two teenage sons, quoted in E Dowler and C Calvert, *Nutrition and Diet in Lone-parent Families in London*, Family Policy Studies Centre for the Joseph Rowntree Foundation, 1995, p35

6 S Middleton, K Ashworth and I Braithwaite, *Small Fortunes: Spending on Children*, Childhood Poverty and Parental Sacrifice, Joseph Rowntree Foundation, 1997

7 Woman, commenting on shopping for food, quoted in P Beresford, D Green, R Lister and K Woodard, *Poverty First Hand: poor people speak for themselves*, CPAG, 1999, p94

8 Long-term income support claimants (lone parents), and couple on low wages, quoted in B Dobson, A Beardsworth, T Keil and R Walker, *Diet, Choice and Poverty: Social, cultural and nutritional aspects of food consumption among low income families*, Family Policy Studies Centre with the Joseph Rowntree Foundation, 1994, p24

9 Couples on income support, quoted in B Dobson, A Beardsworth, T Keil and R Walker, *Diet, Choice and Poverty: Social, cultural and nutritional aspects of food consumption among low income families*, Family Policy Studies Centre with the Joseph Rowntree Foundation, 1994, p18

10 See note 6

11 Lone parents on income support, interviewed for E Dowler and C Calvert, *Nutrition and Diet in Lone-parent Families in London*, Family Policy Studies Centre for the Joseph Rowntree Foundation, 1995

12 B Dobson, A Beardsworth, T Keil and R Walker, *Diet, Choice and Poverty: Social, cultural and nutritional aspects of food consumption among low income families*, Family Policy Studies Centre with the Joseph Rowntree Foundation, 1994, p17

13 B Dobson, A Beardsworth, T Keil and R Walker, *Diet, Choice and Poverty: Social, cultural and nutritional aspects of food consumption among low income families*, Family Policy Studies Centre with the Joseph Rowntree Foundation, 1994

5 WHAT IS HAPPENING TO ADDRESS FOOD POVERTY?

Food poverty is of course not new, but since the 1950s [...] it has been a 'Cinderella' subject within public policy [...] it has been a kind of 'second division' subject in social policy.[1]

POLICY CONTEXT

Food poverty at last shows evidence of having been promoted from the second division of policy issues so that food permeates and is to be found or mentioned in many debates, including those on health, inequalities, education and social exclusion. Early in the twentieth century, professionals and some politicians worried about whether poor people had enough to eat, and during the 'Hungry Thirties' questions were asked in the House of Commons about dietary standards and the cost of providing sufficient means to live. These debates were serious, and recognised the consequences of setting the wrong levels for wage legislation and National Assistance for men, women, and particularly, children.[2] At the beginning of the twenty-first century, rich countries in Europe, the US and Canada face the same questions. Do people have enough money to eat properly, and if not, what can be done about it?

What should be the premise for any intervention? By and large, the driving forces so far have been either welfare support or development of human capital. Welfare was, and is, provided for those who have been unable to provide for themselves, or for whom the market has failed to supply the means of adequate living. Indeed, the term 'welfare foods' is used to refer to food distributed to people seen to be in special need, either because of their age (eg, children) and/or their physiological state (eg, pregnancy), or because they did not have enough money from work or a pension to feed themselves (eg, income support claimants). In Britain, the welfare food scheme, set up in 1940, was originally a universal provision to protect pregnant women and children as part of the war effort. It was subsequently targeted to the economically vulnerable, defined by social security provision.[3] One reason why mothers and babies are protected is because they represent crucial 'human capital': children are the workers of the future, they have to grow well, be healthy and strong, and have to be able to take advantage of education, so they need to be fed properly. Similarly, expectant mothers need to produce healthy children, and all adults need good food to be able to work productively. The productivity argument is not much used in Britain today, although it is still important in many poorer parts of the world.[4]

An important underlying assumption behind much intervention in nutrition in Britain has been nutritional or housekeeping ignorance – that people did not know how to budget or cook properly. Policy responses have often therefore to try to teach people appropriate knowledge and skills. But in practice these policies have had only limited success. The causes of food poverty are more fundamental and structural, so need appropriate structural response. Whether or not the activities of the present Government represent a real policy shift remains to be seen.

> Few human rights have been endorsed with such frequency, unanimity or urgency as the right to food, yet probably no other human right has been so comprehensively and systematically violated on such a wide scale in recent decades.[5]

In contrast to the welfare/human capital responses, the United Nations agencies argue the need to recognise that access to sufficient, safe, appropriate food is a human right. Such a recognition, which would build on the food security arguments of Chapter 1, leads to different sorts of policy response.[6] A human rights framework differs from goals stated by government in that it imposes obligation, not recommended options, on the state and carries with it civil and political rights, which must be implemented in practice. Such a framework transfers food poverty from a 'needs' approach to a 'rights' approach, which has implications in national and European law, and introduces accountability. Finally, it implies a normative basis to responses rather than safety–net or emergency. A human rights framework would require the obligation to:

- **respect** access to adequate food under all circumstances for everyone, which in turn would mean guaranteeing everyone has sufficient income, or means of obtaining income (work, pension, etc) to meet basic food needs recognised as appropriate in a given society;
- **protect** food access, which includes a responsibility to ensure that private institutions or individuals do not deprive others of their access to adequate food;
- **fulfil** the right whenever individuals or groups are unable to feed themselves. Examples might include homeless people who use voluntary sector day centres to obtain sufficient food from their benefit, or homeless and temporarily housed parents with young children in bed and breakfast accommodation, who live with inadequate food preparation facilities and so have to purchase take-away food and sandwiches. Another would be refugees or asylum seekers, faced with voucher schemes to obtain food which are inadequate in provision and amount.

This approach has not yet gained much support in Britain. Some voluntary sector groups are picking up on social justice in relation to food, and some local primary care trust partnerships have used a rights approach.[7] In the main, the human right to food and its implications for policy has been ignored.

In this chapter we review what is currently being done to address food poverty in Europe, nationally and locally. We begin by examining key policy statements and their potential to generate change.

POLICY STATEMENTS AT THE EUROPEAN LEVEL

WORLD HEALTH ORGANIZATION EUROPEAN OFFICE

In the past, the World Health Organization (WHO) has shown only limited interest in nutrition as a component of public health, and little attention has been paid to the nutritional or food security needs of low income groups in Europe. Recently, however, there has been a change of focus, and there is now an emphasis on understanding the needs of those who experience food insecurity as well as exploring the policy implications.

In November 1999, at a meeting of representatives from the 51 member states, the WHO European Office acknowledged the role that food inequalities play in contributing to mortality throughout the region. This stance has been highlighted in an Action Plan for Food and

Nutrition Policy, endorsed by members in September 2000.[8] The Action Plan stresses the complementarity of different sectors in formulating and implementing policies aimed at improving:

- food safety (which is where much energy and money is currently being spent);
- nutrition for low income groups throughout the life cycle;
- a sustainable, equitable food supply.

> The Action Plan also highlights the need to assess the public health impact of an increasingly globalised economy, and that this must include both the food economy, and the nutritional consequences of globalisation. The UK has signed up to this Action Plan, as a member state.

EUROPEAN UNION FRENCH PRESIDENCY INITIATIVE

In 2000, the French assumed presidency of the European Union (EU) and chose to highlight the importance of human nutrition as a major determinant of health. The report and resolution for European action was accepted by the Council of Ministers in December 2000.[9] The report stresses the critical role food and nutrition play in maintaining (or damaging) public health, and the economic and social costs of ignoring them. It specifically refers to the discrepancies in wealth within member states and marked increases in poverty levels across the EU12 between the late 1980s and early 1990s. It states that:

> access to an affordable, safe and varied healthy diet and to health promoting physical activity is a significant factor in these [mortality] inequalities. [...] Money is obviously fundamental, as are the circumstance and environment in which poorer people live. [...] Poverty, which affects a variable proportion of individuals and families in the EU, poses a major constraint on access to quality foodstuffs. This only serves to increase the social exclusion of the poor. (pp21, 23)

The report endorses the principle of subsidiarity: that EU member states are primarily responsible for developing and carrying out nutrition and food policies, with EU policy giving added value. Dietary diversity and cultural identity is to be respected, as is the possibility of free and informed choice for all the population. A strong scientific basis for policies is encouraged. Significantly, the final statement is that the EU nutrition policy should be established in a way that respects social justice, with priority given to influencing access to a nutritious diet for disadvantaged groups. In practice, few instruments for implementation are identified in the policy document, other than urging access to fruit and vegetables. However, the fact that food poverty is both recognised as undesirable, and seen as an EU responsibility, are good beginnings for building alliances for action.

POLICY STATEMENTS AT NATIONAL GOVERNMENT LEVEL

UK LOW INCOME AND DIET PROJECT TEAM: 1994-6

In the early 1990s, a Nutrition Task Force was set up to implement targets and goals in relation to nutrition set out in the strategy for improving the nation's health. The Task Force recognised that 'people on limited incomes may experience particular difficulties in obtaining a healthy and varied diet' but concluded that 'the needs of [low income households] could not be met by national actions [...but] the most effective way to assist people on low incomes [...] is by encouraging effective local initiatives and projects.'[10]

A Low Income and Diet Project Team was set up to 'disseminate examples of good local practice which might enable those on low incomes to ensure they eat a healthy diet'. In other words, the policy premise was that it was up to individuals and local communities to deal with their own problems. No acknowledgement was made of larger structural or material factors and responsibilities. The Project Team's terms of reference explicitly excluded comment on the adequacy of means-tested benefit levels, and a member of the Department for Social Security was an observer at the meetings to ensure that the Project Team kept to its brief.

In practice, the project team did not focus primarily on individual behaviour, or only on community level activities, but also reviewed the implications of changes in food retailing and the responsibilities of local authorities and national government. Their work drew on the concepts of food and nutrition security, access and entitlement to show the links between income, living conditions and food. The report produced highlighted the need for a national network of local projects and initiatives on food and low income, and called for creation of local public/private sector food partnerships, especially in areas of multiple disadvantage, to regenerate local food economies. Despite the good work of the project team and their subsequent promotion of its recommendations, the report received little media coverage or public attention when it was published in April 1996.

POLICY INITIATIVES UNDER NEW LABOUR SINCE 1997

Our new Government was elected on a dual pledge to rebuild the National Health Service and to tackle the root causes of illness. We are committed to reducing inequalities in health and we shall do so with a clear sense of priorities...to attack the underlying causes of ill health and to break the cycle of social and economic deprivation and social exclusion.

Tessa Jowell, Minister for Public Health, July 1997

SAVING LIVES: OUR HEALTHIER NATION

The publication in 1998 and 1999 of the Green and White Papers *Saving Lives: Our Healthier Nation: a contract for health* signalled a shift in Government and health authority approach.[11] Poverty and deprivation were acknowledged as prime causes of ill health and mortality, and the improvement of the health of the worst off in society was established as a principal aim. Policy documents drew on a summary of research in inequalities in health, known as the Acheson Inquiry, published in late 1998.[12] Access to food was listed as one of the key factors contributing to health inequalities (the example was of being unable to reach decent supermarkets by public transport), along with the lack of opportunity that people on low incomes have to put their knowledge about what is good for health into practice.

The publication of these papers were promising signs that the structural and social components of poor nutrition were being taken seriously. The Acheson Inquiry recommended 'policies to increase the availability and accessibility of food stuffs to supply an adequate and affordable diet' (p65) and the 'further development of policies which will ensure adequate retail provision of food to those who are disadvantaged' (p66). However, in practice, these proposals for policy appeared within the White Paper not as calls for structural change in retail provision, or levels of living through redistributive measures, but as recommendations to promote community food projects. The agenda overall had widened to some extent: partnerships, long term commitment to community development, and integrated national government policy, were highlighted as features of the new approach to public health. The solution to poverty, and food poverty in particular, was not solely the responsibility of those living in and with poverty, although they certainly seemed to have a large part to play.

THE NHS PLAN

The NHS Plan, published in 2000, makes particular mention of the need to increase fruit and vegetable consumption, through improving the availability and affordability at local levels.[13] It states that: 'People make their own choices about what to eat. The role of Government is to ensure people have information and proper access to healthy food wherever they live' (p110). Among commitments for action by 2004 are:

● reform of welfare foods programme to ensure children in poverty have access to a healthy diet, and increased support for breastfeeding and parenting;
● a new National School Fruit Scheme, where every child in nursery and aged 4-6 in infant schools will be entitled to a free piece of fruit each school day (following pilot studies);
● a 'five-a-day' programme to increase fruit and vegetable consumption;
● work with the retail industry and producers to increase provision and access through local initiatives and co-operatives.

SOCIAL EXCLUSION UNIT REPORT ON NATIONAL NEIGHBOURHOOD RENEWAL STRATEGY

Another important policy development was the publication in late 1998 of the Social Exclusion Unit Report: *Bringing Britain Together: A national strategy for neighbourhood renewal*.[14] In it, a national strategy to reduce the gap between the poorest neighbourhoods and the rest of the country was set out. Its critical aims were:

● to invest in people, rather than buildings;
● to involve communities in planning and managing decisions;
● to build skills and neighbourhood institutions, rather than parachuting in professionals with short-term solutions;
● to sustain long-term political commitment to integrated policies.

It sought lessons from good practice at the local level. Eighteen cross-cutting Action Teams were created as a fast-track contribution to the policy making process. Three were particularly pertinent to food: *Community Self-help* (No 9: to encourage and strengthen volunteering); *Schools Plus* (No 11: to support homework centres, breakfast clubs and summer schools); and *Shops* (No 13: to identify best practice and innovative approaches to improving poor neighbourhoods' access to food and services).

The Policy Action Team 13 Report was discussed in Chapter 2. It was published in late 1999, as a draft, consultation document.[15] It reviewed problems of food access and outlined potential responses at national and local levels, and from the private and voluntary sectors. The PAT 13 Report mainly concentrated on community based retailing strategies and small businesses. It made useful recommendations about what could be done to support, strengthen and improve small businesses and to encourage or enable local communities to work in partnerships, or at least to make more use of, local small stores. The report recommended setting up local task forces to support viable local, accessible retail opportunities. To date, little central Government activity has followed, and no central mechanism has been created or even mooted to co-ordinate responses.

In January 2001 a report based on 30 months' consultation by the Social Exclusion Unit neighbourhood renewal team was published.[16] It highlighted achievements over the previous three years and set quantified targets for improving the most deprived neighbourhoods in England, so as to 'make them places where people will want to live and work'. Similar publications are being released for Scotland and Wales. This time there is no mention of access to shops or appropriate food: the issue seems to have dropped from the regeneration agenda again.

SCOTTISH EXECUTIVE

A number of initiatives are planned, including the appointment of a National Diet Action Co-ordinator, to implement some of the recommendations of the Scottish Diet Action Plan.[17] They will work with manufacturers, retailers and caterers to improve the quality and nutritional content of food, and with partnership agencies to promote general changes in consumer attitudes to healthy food. CPAG in Scotland is leading a campaign to provide free and nutritious school meals to all children.[18] A bill, drafted in consultation with 20 organisations, was launched through the Scottish Parliament in June 2001, and signed by 12 MSPs from five political parties. Currently, it is being considered by Scottish parliamentary staff with regard to the parliamentary standing orders and once approved it can be formally published and will begin its process through the Scottish Parliament.

NATIONAL ACTIVITIES AND RESPONSES

The current Government has acknowledged the injustice and economic inefficiency of current inequalities in health and of social exclusion and has encouraged innovative, creative thinking across traditional sectoral boundaries to address them in the long and short term. Local food projects are being promoted in national policy documents and through local Health Action Zone plans, and anti-poverty activities, and by non-governmental organisations such as Sustain and Oxfam UK. These and other specific policy initiatives aimed at improving food security for low income families are outlined in this section.

DEPARTMENT OF HEALTH AND DEPARTMENT FOR EDUCATION AND SKILLS

A number of national programmes and schemes aimed at improving diet and nutrition in children and/or families have been launched since the Labour Government came to power in 1997. These have been produced for England, Scotland, Wales and Northern Ireland. Many cut across departmental or professional boundaries, although in practice one or other department usually takes the lead. Many of these initiatives present local groups with the opportunities to tender for pump-priming funding and support, provided they adhere to the stated policy goals. For example, Health Action Zones and Education Action Zones are area based partnerships between local agencies, including local authorities and health authorities, where local strategies to address local problems are carried out using central extra funding. Action Zone status is won by competitive tender; most early successes are concentrated in deprived areas. Local food initiatives, particularly food co-ops, community cafes and school breakfast clubs, are often highlighted in the bids and proposed activities. Similarly, Sure Start is an area based cross-government initiative involving agencies at local and national level working together to improve services for young children under four years old and their families, in areas of disadvantage. Again, community based food and nutrition initiatives are often included as part of these initiatives.

These policy initiatives are evaluated elsewhere, but one challenge is that evidence shows area based actions have limited success in addressing household or neighbourhood deprivation.[19] More critically, few Health Action Zones or Health Improvement Programmes have explicit targets for reducing inequalities in children's health; fewer, if any, mention food or nutrition. Many of the community based initiatives encouraged by national policy are heavily dependent on volunteer labour and short-term, start-up funding.

BOX 5.1: 'Give me 5': Five-a-day Pilot Project to reduce cancer in Sandwell

Sandwell Health Authority in the West Midlands has been chosen as a Department of Health pilot site to try and reduce cancer, as well as heart disease and stroke, by making it easier for residents to eat five portions of fruit and vegetables a day. During 2000/1, £96,000 of central money is being spent driving home the message and improving the means. A new home delivery service, run by Sandwell Community Foods, will enable people in more deprived areas with a very limited range of foods in local shops, to buy high quality, low cost fruit and vegetables on their doorsteps. This should become self-financing after a year. Bulk purchasing schemes and 'sale or return' agreements for small local retailers have been developed with Sandwell Community Foods, whose Food Project Manager said: 'Many retailers simply can't afford to risk stocking fruit and vegetables – whereas chocolate and crisps have a much longer shelf life. Our aim is to make it possible for them to stock a good range of fresh produce.' Sandwell Community Foods (which began life ten years ago as a volunteer run food co-op) is also providing free and low cost fruit to schools in areas of high deprivation for 'fruit only' tuck shops, which makes the schools eligible for a healthy tuck shop award and £200 worth of free sports equipment. A campaign bus has hit the road, to take the 'five-a-day' messages round the borough and give live cooking and tasting sessions. The Health Authority is planning six 'five-a-day' award winning cafes.[20]

Sandwell Health Authority is unusual in having a Food Policy Advisor in Health Promotion whose job is to initiate and co-ordinate improving food access for poor families. He is also measuring how difficult it is to buy a healthy balanced diet within walking distance of where people live, and producing baseline maps of food access to monitor change, using methods piloted in London.[21] The Sandwell project is a good example of a local authority and health authority activity which is taking advantage of national initiatives to provide pump-priming money and technical support to target food poverty.

The Department of Health has two current nutrition initiatives being piloted in areas of high deprivation. Neither is specifically aimed at reducing food poverty, but both aim to improve access to fresh fruit and vegetables. In one, a national programme is testing the feasibility of preventing colorectal (bowel) cancer through increasing consumption of fruit and vegetables. Two-year contracts in five areas of England have been issued, to pilot and evaluate different approaches.

The other Department of Health initiative is the National School Fruit Scheme, being piloted in 2000/01 in over 20 areas and many schools through Health Action Zones. It entitles every child aged four to six to a free piece of fruit each school day. The policy document stresses the complementarity of the scheme with work in the National Curriculum in schools, and the Healthy Schools Programme.[22] Key features of successful programmes are outlined in the policy document. Evaluation will identify effective ways to implement the scheme with minimum disruption and burden to schools. The scheme will be rolled out nationally to all children aged four to six in primary schools by 2004. By summer 2001, the Department of Health estimated that over 80,000 school children in 548 schools, in 27 areas, were receiving free fruit each school day. Evaluation results from the early pilot studies, and reaction from schools, have been very positive.[23]

> The Government believes that every one should have access to healthy food, and that children in particular need a better chance of a healthy start in life. [...] That is why we are introducing the National School Fruit Scheme, which will entitle our youngest school children to free fruit each day. Alongside new nutritional standards for school meals, and community projects to improve access to healthy food, this is a vital step towards improving all children's health and tackling health inequalities across the country.

(from the Ministers' foreword to the National School Fruit Scheme)

HEALTHY SCHOOLS INITIATIVE

Launched in May 1998, the Healthy Schools Initiative was a response to the White Papers *Excellence in Schools* and *Saving Lives – Our Healthier Nation*. It is jointly funded by the Department of Health and the Department for Education and Skills, to raise awareness of all involved in schools, including the wider community, of opportunities to improve health. The 'whole school' approach, and project examples of good practice, are promoted. Provision of food, as well as how food is dealt with in the curriculum, was seen as ideally part of such a whole school approach. Food provision in schools covers a whole range, including the food served during the school day (lunches and at break times) as well as food served prior to and after school, for example, breakfast and homework clubs run on school premises.

> Healthy schools need healthy school meals. That's not about making school meals boring or stopping children from enjoying what they eat. But it is about applying some imagination to make sure children can enjoy what they eat and that what they eat is good for them.
>
> *Tessa Jowell, Minister of Health, DfEE, 1998*

Establishing what and how food is served in school meals is a complex process that involves government, local education authorities, schools, caterers, teachers, parents and, most importantly, the pupils. The recent legislation on food based nutritional standards have to be set in the context of other changes in Government policy, such as delegation of responsibility for school meals in all secondary schools [24] and those primary schools that want to do so. Schools now have much greater control and responsibility for the provision of food in the dining room. It is therefore important that nutritional standards are easy for LEAs, schools and caterers to apply and to monitor – the stated reason why the Government introduced food based nutrition standards for school meals rather than the nutrient based standards advocated by a number of groups and organisations.[25]

The logistics of serving food in schools requires careful planning and discipline. First, the numbers involved may be large – over 1,000 in a large secondary school. Second, the time available for serving, allowing pupils to choose food and eat it, is limited, normally less than one hour. In secondary schools there is little time for pupils to calculate the cost of the foods selected and this can cause difficulties for those with little money or who are entitled to a free meal and therefore have a fixed amount to spend. Young people frequently say they choose chips because they are cheap and they 'fill you up'. Third, the numbers of children having meals vary from day to day and from season to season – summer is a popular time for packed lunches to be eaten outside. Fourth, the budget for supplying food is a very tight one – particularly with the rapid uptake of school budget delegation – allowing little scope for mistakes and/or wastage. Finally, there is competition from packed lunches, local shops and cafes. The whole process can be daunting for caterers and diners alike, particularly for small children.[26]

The actual food served in school meals obviously varies between different schools and individual caterers. Increasingly schools are setting up School Nutrition Action Groups (SNAGs) as part of Healthy Schools Initiatives.[27] SNAGs involve those involved in school lunches or in a position to advise on the meals, including caterers, pupils, teachers, school governors and dieticians. SNAGs make decisions on what food should be served and priced, on the presentation of food and on improving the dining areas. Even in schools where SNAGs have not been set up caterers normally discuss menus with head teachers and respond to feedback. Schools without a SNAG may have a Schools Council – a forum which allows pupils to air their views about the running of the school – that may press for changes to be made to school meals. Such initiatives may also be taken by school governors or parent teacher associations.

Schools have been encouraged to set up breakfast clubs. In July 1999 the Department of Health and the Department for Education and Employment announced funding support for piloting breakfast clubs, particularly in areas of deprivation. Evaluation is being conducted by a team from the University of East Anglia. The three aims of this initiative are:

- to provide a free breakfast for children who arrive at school having had nothing to eat;
- to offer healthy choices;
- to establish a positive start of the school day, helping to reduce lateness or truancy, and improving attitudes, behaviour and motivation to learn.

Many teachers and parents have reported informally that breakfast clubs they know or run seem to be achieving these aims – see Box 5.2. However, they also report facing similar problems to other community food projects, such as:

- maintaining funding;
- maintaining volunteer support;
- difficulties for schools with no catering facilities and non systematic attendance, which makes evaluating the impact on individuals difficult.

BOX 5.2: **Breakfast clubs in schools**

White Hart Lane Secondary School and Park View Academy Secondary School in Haringey, and Raynham Primary School in Enfield, are taking part in the Department of Health breakfast club pilot scheme. The clubs have run since late 1999, with limited, one-off funding to start the projects. Pupils and parents were told that the school would only be able to offer free breakfasts for a limited period, to avoid disappointment once the funding had run out. Young people were offered a range of healthy eating options, such as toast, cereal, fresh fruit and fruit juice. About 70-100 pupils took advantage of these offered goodies at each school every day. White Hart Lane School has opened its library from 8.00 am to coincide with the breakfast club. Initial feedback has revealed a reduction in lateness as well as improved concentration among pupils.[28]

DEPARTMENT OF HEALTH AND DEPARTMENT OF SOCIAL SECURITY

The Welfare Food Scheme is under review. The Scheme provision is currently targeted at those claiming income support or income based jobseeker's allowance, providing pregnant or breastfeeding women and children aged 1-5 years with a voucher which can be exchanged for one pint of whole or semi-skimmed milk a day (or four litres a week). They are also entitled to a Department of Health vitamin supplement. Also under this scheme, non-breastfed children under one year can have 900g infant formula a week and a vitamin supplement. Some non-breastfed infants whose parents claim working families' tax credit can also purchase 900g infant formula a week at a reduced cost from maternity and child health clinics. Milk entitlement operates through tokens exchanged at appropriate shops; vitamins are obtained from clinics. In addition, children under five years attending scheme-registered day care facilities can receive a third of a pint of milk a day.[29]

In November 1999, the Welfare Food Scheme Review Group accepted a draft report, with the following comments and recommendations:

- the scheme offers significant economic and nutritional benefits to low income households, and is potentially very important in improving the health of vulnerable mothers and young children;
- uptake of vitamin supplements, regarded as a simple, cost-effective intervention, is very low; improved systems of provision are needed;
- uptake of milk is very high. Most mothers use tokens to obtain infant formula, reflecting very low breastfeeding rates among low income households. About 50 per cent of children in day care

attend facilities registered with the scheme; some of these children may receive excessive milk if they also receive scheme milk at home. Reduction in currently excess volume of formula for those over six months in favour of provisions to promote timely complementary feeding would be appropriate. Extension of formula provision to older children would reduce iron deficiency prevalence;

• amendments to the current package include choices other than milk, and improved composition of vitamin supplements to pregnant women; breastfeeding incentives; reduction in liquid cow's milk to children under one year;

• free vitamin supplements should be extended to children from minority ethnic groups;

• the disability living allowance should take account of the special nutritional needs of children in low income families that are not currently met by a daily pint of cow's milk.

The *Welfare Food Report* highlights current innovative small-scale schemes operating in parts of the country, such as the Govan Milk Token Initiative (see Box 5.3).

COMMUNITY BASED ACTIVITIES AND RESPONSES

COMMUNITY FOOD PROJECTS

During the years when previous governments denied the existence of food poverty, or laid blame on individuals for mismanagement, those struggling to live with the reality had to tackle the immediate problems in practical ways. Often professionals took the initiative: a community dietician, an enlightened GP, a local priest, a concerned head teacher, would lend time and skills to helping set up a 'community café' where local people could meet and eat cheaply, or a food co-op where (usually) fruit and vegetables bought through a wholesaler or market using economies of scale could be bagged up and sold at a low price. In some instances, projects were started up by local people themselves. Many projects began as genuine partnerships between local families and professional(s). Table 5.1 describes typical types of community food projects and their basic requirements. Much more detail can be obtained from the Sustain/Health Development Agency (see Box 5.4) and Scottish Community Diet Project networks (see Box 5.5).

BOX 5.3: **Milk token initiative – Govan, Glasgow**

If a family on income support or income-based Jobseeker's allowance includes:
- a pregnant woman;
- a child under five years old,

they are entitled to a fresh milk token which can be exchanged in designated shops for four litres or seven pints of whole/semi-skimmed cow's milk a week.

If a child is breastfed, the mother can drink the milk herself. Alternatively, bottle fed babies under one year can receive 900g formula baby milk a week by obtaining a dried milk token instead. In addition, they are all entitled to a Department of Health vitamin supplement from the clinic.

A system was set up in Govan, Glasgow, to enable families on income support to get their free milk entitlement and to encourage them to eat more fruit and vegetables.

A community group can operate as a milk co-operative and register with the Welfare Food Reimbursement Unit as an approved liquid milk supplier. The Unit reimburses the milk co-op for milk supplied. Any difference between this reimbursement price and the actual cost of milk is a profit, which accrues to the milk co-op. They return this profit to members weekly as a 'healthy dividend', which parents collect when they come to hand in their tokens and buy extra milk. They get their milk, and the healthy dividend: a bag of fruit and vegetables. In practice, this dividend bag of fruit and vegetables worth £1 wholesale may be worth double this at local retail prices.

The report of the Low Income and Diet Project Team made clear local projects, while important in their own terms, cannot provide the comprehensive coverage and integrated solutions to the depth and extent of food poverty at regional and national level. The problem was simply too big. Local, community based projects lack funds for long term development, are often isolated in activity, and rely heavily on volunteers.

However, community based food initiatives still seem an attractive option to policy makers, professionals in health and regeneration, and to local people themselves. Community projects can help to overcome social isolation, give people a sense of worth and increase a feeling of wellbeing. They can also help in raising levels of skills and training, enable individuals to take more control of their own health and welfare, as well as promoting healthier eating. They are seen as a way of achieving change in the short term. Local projects can contribute to raising the 'social capital' of a community. Many of these aspects of community food projects have tended to be overlooked in the past.

TABLE 5.1: Types of community based food projects

'Cook and Eat'

- weekly sessions (usually) for a set number of weeks, during which regulars prepare simple, low cost dishes for a meal, which they share together before leaving
- sometimes aimed at children, linked to a local school
- tend to be run by health professionals
- costs/needs: equipment, fuel, food, hall, kitchen

Food co-op

- usually held weekly; usually for fresh fruit and vegetables, sometimes dried goods, 'soup packs', recipes too
- people place weekly orders which are collated, purchased and packed by volunteers; people pay for orders on collection; sometimes run like a shop
- tend to be started/run by community development professionals
- costs/needs: vehicle and/or petrol, weighing scales, bags, hall

Community cafés

- cafés serving meals, drinks, snacks at low prices; people can stay long periods; sometimes aimed at children or older people
- sometimes have church links or located where other services on offer, such as advice, family support, clothes
- tend to be started/run by development or health professionals
- costs/needs: site, equipment, food, food hygiene, cooking and business skills, hall

Food growing

- people learn or are enabled to grow their own food in community gardens or allotments
- sometimes linked to food co-ops, schools
- tend to be started/run by development professionals
- costs/needs: site, fencing, equipment, seed, inputs

Food provision

- diverse activities involving building based meal provision
- breakfast/after school clubs provide food to school children
- day centre free cooked meals, sometimes untargeted (anyone can come) sometimes targeted by age (older people)
- tend to be run by education professionals, or faith groups, or concerned citizens; sometimes local authority provision
- costs/needs: hall, equipment, food

Partnerships

- partnership is a loose term for projects with links to retailers, which can be financial, more likely to be business skills
- include community shops, food co-ops
- tend to be started/run by development professionals

Source: P McGlone, B Dobson, E Dowler and M Nelson, *Food projects and how they work*, York Publishing for the Joseph Rowntree Foundation, 1999

The networks set up by Sustain and the Scottish Community Diet Project described below have been important in helping many to find ways round some of the problems they face.

Local food projects are a disparate set of activities, seen in different ways by different people investing in them; despite the lists in Table 5.1, they are difficult to define, and to characterise systematically in terms of activities, management structure and approach, all of which vary. Recent empirical research funded by the Joseph Rowntree Foundation investigated the sustainability of food projects and the policy implications for those with responsibility for managing professionals, initiating collaborative community based ventures, or securing or releasing funding.[30] The research drew on the experiences from 25 different projects, from different areas and settings throughout England, Wales and Scotland. What was clear was that no single formula for management or structure seemed to guarantee success. However, food projects functioned best when their activities were in a context or setting with which local people identified.

The process of setting up a project was seldom simple and straightforward; it had often been a complex and frustrating process, driven by many factors outside the control of the people involved. Projects where solutions had been 'parachuted in' particularly failed to get off the ground. Some projects continue for many years, carrying out the same activities. Others go through cycles of regenerating themselves, or evolving into new sets of activities, in response to external factors, such as loss or gain of professionals, and new funding initiatives.

The key factors affecting sustainability of local food projects can be summed up as:

- project credibility with local people, shared ownership and responsiveness to local needs, and a means of reconciling the different agendas of professionals, volunteers and members/users;
- access to ongoing, sustainable funding, rather than a succession of short-term 'start-up' funding;
- generation and maintenance of true support from community members and a range of professionals as necessary;
- being realistic about time, both how long it would take a project to get going (longer than most people anticipated), and the amount of time people themselves had to give;
- energy and commitment from key workers (whether paid or voluntary).

THE SUCCESS OF FOOD PROJECTS

Do local food projects 'work'? Most of those involved usually argue that they succeed in meeting their own aims and objectives, despite almost universal problems with funding continuity. Professionals, volunteers and 'users' tend to judge success differently; this is a challenge to funders and facilitators who want consistent, simple outcome indicators. Numbers of users is often quoted, although these can vary from as few as six for a weekly 'cook and eat' session, to 150 people a day using a café. Projects attracting low numbers are often operating at their space or equipment capacity or are working in areas of multiple needs where participation is more difficult to sustain. Numbers and project duration are important indicators for those running projects: engaging local people's interest and commitment is a critical factor in 'success', best served by adopting a broad agenda. This works against establishing the kind of focused, hard outcomes desired by funders and managers.

Some projects do try to assess changes in users' eating habits, and usually show they have had some, if not a large, effect. But many argue that the social gains at individual and community levels should not be separated from nutritional objectives but intrinsic to their achievement. Food projects should not be judged solely on whether they can produce changes in nutrition or health outcomes measured over the long-term (such as changes in blood vitamin levels), important though these are. Rather, they contribute to changes in short-term nutrition indicators, such as skills and confidence to use a wider range of foodstuffs than before, or to improved food purchasing or eating patterns. But many project workers and volunteers are sceptical that traditional outcome measures, such as measurable changes in the consumption of fruit and vegetables, or improvement in nutrient intakes, accurately reflect positive achievements, arguing that success is ultimately about satisfying the interests of the different groups involved, rather than meeting targets imposed from outside. Again, this is quite a challenge to external funders and managers.

> Local people and organisations can easily identify the problems they face and propose solutions. Very often, these solutions cannot be implemented because of the inflexibility of centrally devised programmes and policies. The main obstacles to effective co-ordination at a local level are narrowly defined value for money and other performance indicators; rigid admini-

> stration so that local actors are not empowered to vire expenditure be-
> tween sub programmes or areas; inflexibility in the face of changing needs.
> National Housing Federation, quoted in the Social Exclusion Unit
> Report, 1998

It is often hard to define the boundaries of community food projects: how much is simply an extension of a professional's job, but with separate funding and demanding a different role? Sometimes 'food projects' in fact contain more than a single activity; sometimes other activities where a 'food project' is physically located can also affect nutritional outcomes although not necessarily defined as the 'project'. Many 'food projects' have aims and activities which extend beyond simply improving food access or food security for people who need them. This can be a strength: the recent policy shift signals change from an exclusive demand for value-for-money, hard outcomes, delivered in the short term, to a recognition that sustainability and participation, shared ownership and capacity building are key to reducing inequalities and deprivation. The interest in 'what works': what enables initiatives to get off the ground, to become sustainable, to adapt and move on, and what are appropriate ways to measure effectiveness and sustainability, fits well with the experience of community initiatives in food.

NATIONAL NETWORKS OF COMMUNITY FOOD ACTIVITIES

The Low Income and Diet Project Team report highlighted the need for a national network of local projects and initiatives working on food and low income. The National Food Alliance (now Sustain: the alliance for food and farming) took on the challenge and, with the Health Education Authority (now Health Development Agency), set up a database for local food projects, and produces a regular newsletter (see Box 5.4). At the same time, the Scottish Community Diet Project was set up in Scotland, following the recommendations of the Scottish Diet Action Plan, also published in 1996 (see Box 5.5).

SURPLUS FOOD REDISTRIBUTION

So-called 'surplus food' redistribution schemes exist to ensure that food which cannot be sold through the normal retailing channels are redistributed to people in need, or who have poor access to food, via

---

BOX 5.4: **Food Poverty Network**

The National Food Alliance (which merged to become Sustain in 1999) set up a food and low income working party in 1988, to produce reports and campaign. In 1994, they published *Food and Low Income – a practical guide for advisers and supporters working with families and young people on low incomes*, written by Suzi Leather and Tim Lobstein. The pack provided information on: diet; hygiene and health; existing food projects; setting up a food project; contacts working in food projects; and food-related benefits. It has been widely used, along with reports of a series of conferences around the country on food and low income. In late 1995, sales of the pack and a grant from the National Lotteries Charities Board enabled the Food Poverty Network to be set up, to provide:

- a quarterly newsletter – *Let us eat cake!* which keeps members in contact, and provides news of funding, campaigns, national policy developments, events and publications;
- a comprehensive database of contacts, with the Health Education Authority (now Health Development Agency) which is available on the internet at www.food.poverty.hda-online.org.uk or telephone 020 7413 1995;
- a 'toolkit' to provide detailed information on how to set up and develop projects;
- challenges to myths about food poverty, and to improve understanding and raise awareness of food poverty;
- a forum for project workers, researchers and campaign groups for sharing information and momentum to create appropriate policies to tackle food poverty.

Since 1999, the Food Poverty Network has co-ordinated a pioneering Community Mapping Project, which enables local people and professionals to understand their local food economies and develop relevant solutions to the problems that prevent them from having access to a healthy diet. Contact: Sustain, 94 White Lion Street, London N1 9PF

---

homeless projects, schools, the Salvation Army or local authority projects.[31] This food includes: perishable products which are at their sell-by, but not their use-by, date; non-perishable processed foods with a long shelf life which are mislabelled, or in faulty packaging, or out-of-date promotions, or cancelled orders near the sell-by date; agricultural products taken off the market to stabilise prices. These foods are not 'unfit for human consumption' in any way. The main schemes for redistribution in the UK are Crisis Fareshare, which collects from supermarkets and delivers to homeless people, and Grocery Aid (formerly Provision), an Institute of Grocery Distribution charitable scheme for food industry support to voluntary sector free food distribution. There are other, local systems in operation, and direct

---

BOX 5.5: **Scottish Community Diet Project (SCDP)**

The SCDP was set up in October 1996, under the auspices of the Scottish Consumer Council, *'to promote and focus dietary initiatives within low-income communities and to bring these within a strategic framework'*. It set out to address practical obstacles to healthy eating by:

- encouraging and enabling community-based activities;
- operating a grant-making system for community initiatives;
- facilitating information exchange and networking (eg, paying for low income community members to attend conferences and meetings in other countries);
- developing models of interagency partnerships between communities and statutory, voluntary, academic and commercial sectors;
- developing methods for local communities to participate in national policy debates;
- exploring strategic issues which could inform and influence policy debates.

It has three full time members of staff and receives funding from the Scottish Executive Department of Health. It publishes a regular newsletter, *Fare Choice*, obtainable free from: Scottish Community Diet Project, c/o SCC, Royal Exchange House, 100 Queen St, Glasgow G1 3DN, or from their website: www.dietproject.co.uk

---

store-charity liaisons. In addition, the Intervention Board is the Government agency responsible for withdrawal and redistribution of surplus agricultural produce under the EU Surplus Food Scheme.

Drop-in day centres, where cooked food (usually) is provided daily, either for free or at a nominal charge, and other food distribution to the homeless, marginally housed and vulnerable, has been a huge growth industry throughout the 1990s. Over 3,000 tonnes of food are distributed in Britain to people in need each year via more than 500 charities.[32] This constitutes more than 160,000 meals a week, at a total direct cost of over £1 million. Across Europe as a whole, increasing numbers of people make use of food banks; *'a centralized warehouse or clearing house registered as a non-profit organization for collecting, storing and distributing surplus food, free of charge, to front-line agencies which provide supplementary food and meals to the hungry'*.[33] There is a strong tradition of promoting the use of food banks in the US and Canada as a strategy for dealing with inequality.[34] The approach seems to be spreading in Europe, with the proliferation of such institutions. In Britain, food banks are not yet widespread, although they are growing, and the ideas seem attractive in some quarters.

BOX 5.6: **Small change for healthy children**

Who says children won't eat fruit? Who says parents don't care? The experience of an East London school says otherwise. Ben Jonson School in Stepney has been participating in a programme called *Small Change*. *Small Change*, run by the charity Global Action Plan, works with primary schools to increase awareness of health and environmental issues and to encourage participation by families in local initiatives.

With Ben Jonson the project promoted healthy snacks and set up a fruit tuck shop. A dietician ran sessions on healthy snacks and lunchboxes with 120 pupils from years 2 and 3. Not only did pupils try new foods, but they took goodie bags home to practice on their families what they had learned at school. As a result of this work, the fruit tuck shop that has been set up has been enormously popular.

With the support of community dieticians, health promotion specialists and district nurses, the project launched a Parent and Child Health Group in the school. Thirty five parents attended the launch and a core of twelve parents have been attending meetings since. Volunteers at a local food co-operative have been funded to offer parents access to affordable, fresh fruit and vegetables. At the second meeting the co-op sold over £100 of fresh food.

The key ingredients have been an imaginative school, a project process that takes the organisational pressure off the school and an approach that focuses on behaviour changing messages on homes.

However, there are very fundamental issues here which need a wider debate than they usually attract. It is clear that surplus food redistribution is welcomed by those on the 'front-line', faced with feeding needy, hungry people on a daily basis. It seems better that those who need the food should get it, rather than it be destroyed. Yet such schemes perpetuate food insecurity by enabling the problems and experience of hunger in rich societies to remain marginalised. Who bothers about the numbers using day centres if their clients are perceived as 'drug users and winos' – ie, those who are perceived to have brought their problems on themselves? The reality is that the majority of day centre clients are not rough sleepers, and even addictive substance users have rights to food.[35]

Secondly, food banks and the like institutionalise the usage of surplus foods. Supermarkets generally welcome such schemes: they are an alternative to disposing of waste through landfill, on which they have to pay increasing taxes. They also welcome the improved public relations image.

Indeed, this is how Grocery Aid is marketed on the Institute of Grocery Distribution website: 'By supporting Grocery Aid, you demonstrate your company's commitment to the community. You also gain environmental benefits. Why throw quality products into landfill? There is also a 'feel good' factor for your staff to know their company is helping people in need.' (www.igd.com/homepage.asp?Grouping=Industry+Charity). Again, the reality is shifting. In practice, because the large supermarkets' retailing system is increasingly efficient (eg, using electronic point of sale systems), there is less surplus being generated. Instead, supermarkets are asked to donate goods and services (such as warehousing, transport, expertise). Furthermore, the products distributed are usually what the supermarkets want to donate, or have surplus – they are not necessarily what those who are poor and hungry want or need to eat.

Finally, surplus food is a 'handout', largely by the private sector. To what extent is this a good thing, encouraging creative partnerships and self-help; or is it perpetuating dependency and victim status?

SUMMARY

- The United Nations agencies call on member states to recognise access to sufficient, safe, appropriate food as a human right; such a framework transfers the policy context of food poverty from a 'needs' to a 'rights' approach.
- In September 2000 Britain was a member state signatory to the WHO European Region Action Plan for Food and Nutrition Policy, which calls for complementary policy implementation on food safety, nutrition for low income groups and a sustainable, equitable food supply.
- The European Union, under the French presidency in 2000, endorsed food and nutrition as major components of policies to reduce inequalities in health, and that access to a nutritious diet for disadvantaged groups should be a priority.
- A number of policy documents from the New Labour Government acknowledge problems of food access for low income groups, and initiatives include the promotion of local food projects and promotion of fresh fruit and vegetable consumption in schools and the wider community.
- Many communities and schools have set up food initiatives of various types; networks of support are developing; ongoing funding and local credibility and ownership are key issues for sustainability.

● Distribution of 'surplus' food, generated by the retail system, is also increasing, as a means of providing meals for people in immediate need; sustainability, desirability and dependency creation are issues needing wider debate.

NOTES

1 T Lang, 'The need for a food policy', *Benefits*, 24, Jan/Feb, 1999, p1-2
2 B Woolf, 'Poverty Lines and Standards of Living', *Proceedings of the Nutrition Society*, 5, 71-81, 1946; J Boyd Orr, *Food Health and Income: Report on A Survey of Adequacy of Diet in Relation to Income*, Macmillan & Co, 1936
3 COMA, Panel on Maternal and Child Nutrition, *Scientific Review of the Welfare Food Scheme*, Report to the Welfare Food Scheme Review Group, 7th Draft, Department of Health, Committee on Medical Aspects of Food and Nutrition Policy (COMA), 1999
4 M C Latham, 'The relationship of nutrition to productivity and well-being of Workers', in: P Pinstrup-Andersen (ed), *The Political Economy of Food and Nutrition Policies*, Johns Hopkins University Press, 1993; L DeRose, E Messer and S Millman, *Who's Hungry? And How Do We Know? Food shortage, poverty and deprivation*, UNU Press, 1998
5 P Alston, 'International law and the right to food', in: B Harriss-White and R Hoffenburg (eds), *Food: Multidisciplinary perspectives*, Blackwell, 1994
6 E Dowler, E Barlösius, E Feichtinger and B Köhler, 'Poverty, Food and Nutrition', in: B Köhler, E Feichtinger, E Barlösius and E Dowler (eds) *Poverty and Food in Welfare Societies*, Sigma Edition, Berlin, 1997
7 National Children's Bureau; B Owens, *Out of the Frying Pan*, Save the Children Fund, 1997; Aston-Mansfield, *The Right to a Healthy diet: Sustaining the fight against food poverty*, Aston-Mansfield, for the London Borough of Newham and Newham NHS Primary Care Trust, 2001
8 A Robertson, 'WHO tackles food inequalities: Europe's first comprehensive Food and Nutrition Action Plan debate, Malta', *Public Health Nutrition*, 3, 1, 2000, pp99-101; World Health Organization, *The Impact of Food and Nutrition on Public Health. Case for a Food and Nutrition Policy and Action Plan for the WHO European Region 2000-2005*, Food and Nutrition Policy Unit, WHO Regional Office for Europe, 2000
9 Council of the European Communities, *Health and Human Nutrition: Elements for European Action*, French Presidency of the European Union Working Paper and Resolution, 2000 – see website of Société Française de Santé Publique www.sfsp-publichealth.org/europe.html and follow links to the French Presidency report.
10 Department of Health, *Eat Well! Action Plan from the Nutrition Task Force to achieve the Health of the Nation targets on diet and nutrition*, Department of Health, 1994, p32.

11 Department of Health, *Our Healthier Nation: A contract for health*, Green Paper February 1998, Cm 3854, The Stationery Office, 1998; Department of Health, *Saving Lives: Our Healthier Nation*, White Paper July 1999, Cm 4386, The Stationery Office, 1999

12 D Acheson, *Independent Inquiry into Inequalities in Health*, Department of Health, 1998

13 Department of Health, *The NHS Plan*, Cmd Paper no 4818, The Stationery Office, 2000

14 Social Exclusion Unit, *Bringing Britain Together: A national strategy for neighbourhood renewal*, HMSO, 1998

15 Department of Health, *Improving Shopping Access*, Policy Action Team 13, Department of Health, 1999 from: www.cabinet-office.gov.uk/seu/ and follow the links to Policy Action Team reports

16 Social Exclusion Unit, *The New Commitment to Neighbourhood Renewal: National Strategy Action Plan*, The Stationery Office, 2001

17 The Scottish Office, *Eating for Health: A Diet Action Plan for Scotland*, 1996

18 Contact Danny Phillips, CPAG Scotland, Unit 425, Pentagon Centre, Washington Street, Glasgow G3 8AZ

19 H Joshi, R D Wiggins, M Bartley, R Mitchell, S Gleave and K Lynch 'Putting health inequalities on the map: does where you live matter and why?' in: H Graham (ed), *Understanding Health Inequalties*, Open University Press, pp143-155; BMJ REF

20 Sandwell Health Report, *Food pilot may cut cancer: New scheme to boost fruit and veg consumption amoung low income families*, newsletter of Sandwell Health Authority, Winter 2000, p1-2.

21 E Dowler, A Blair, D Rex, A Donkin and C Grundy, *Measuring access to healthy food in Sandwell*, Report to the Sandwell Partnership (Health Action Zone), 2001; A J M Donkin, E Dowler, S J Stevenson and S A Turner, 'Mapping access to food in a deprived area: the development of price and availability indices', *Public Health Nutrition*, 3, 1, 2000, pp31-38; A J M Donkin, E Dowler, S J Stevenson and S A Turner, 'Mapping access to food at a local level', *British Food Journal*, 101, 7, 1999, pp554-562

22 Department of Health, *The National School Fruit Scheme*, Department of Health, 2000 available at www.doh.gov.uk/schoolfruitscheme/

23 Department of Health, *Vision to Reality*, DH, 2001 ref 24104

24 Department for Education and Employment, *Fair Funding: Improving delegation to schools* (May 1998), Consultation Paper, DfEE, 1998

25 I Sharp, *Nutrition Guidelines for School Meals: Report of an Expert Working Group*, The Caroline Walker Trust, 1993

26 S A Turner, B Mayall and M Mauthner, 'One big rush – dinner time at school', *Health Education Journal*, Vol. 54, 1995, pp.18-27.

27 SNAG News: UK newsletter for School Nutrition Action Groups, obtainable from the Health Education Trust, 18 High Street, Broom, Alcester, Warwickshire B50 4HJ

28 Contact Sheena Carr, Health Promotion Department, Enfield and Haringey Health Authority, Holbrook House, Cockfosters Road, Barnet, Hertfordshire EN4 0DR

29 Full details obtainable from DSS, or at www.dss.gov.uk/ba

30 P McGlone, B Dobson, E Dowler and M Nelson, *Food Projects and How They Work*, York Publishing for the Joseph Rowntree Foundation, 1999

31 C Hawkes and J Webster, *Too much and too little? Debates on surplus food redistribution*, Sustain, 2000

32 See note 31

33 G Riches, *Food Banks and the Welfare Crisis*, Canadian Council of Social Development, 1986, p16; G Riches, 'Hunger in Canada: Abandoning the right to food', in: G Riches (ed), *First World Hunger: Food security and welfare politics*, Macmillan Press, 1997

34 G Riches, 'Hunger, food security and welfare politics', *Proceedings of the Nutrition Society*, 56, 1a, 1997, pp63-74; J Poppendieck, 'The USA: Hunger in the Land of Plenty', in: G Riches (ed), *First World Hunger: Food security and welfare politics*, Macmillan Press, 1997

35 N S Evans, '"Eat Well!" – an intervention programme to improve the nutritional value of food provided for homeless and marginalised people', in: B M Köhler, E Feichtinger, E Dowler and G Winkler (eds) *Public Health and Nutrition: The challenge*, Sigma Edition, Berlin, 1999; N S Evans and E Dowler, 'Food, health and eating among single homeless and marginalized people in London', *Journal of Human Nutrition and Dietetics*, 12, 1999, pp179-199

6 NEXT STEPS: THE CHALLENGES FOR ACTION

A fundamental problem with the government's approach to the nation's diet is the apparent assumption that, because poor diets result in disease, methods which are appropriate to tackling disease (especially preventative measures such as health education and health promotion) will be suffic-ient to address this problem... When we have finally exhausted the capacities of individuals and communities to radically alter the Scottish diet we might then turn to address the structural factors that have such an influence in determining the choices we can make.[1]

Families who live for any length of time on low incomes, whether from wages or benefits, face severe problems getting enough food to meet their health and social needs. Many of the problems stem from long term, structural inadequacies that no amount of small-scale, one-off initiatives can solve. Too often, food and nutrition has been relegated to a sideline in regeneration or anti-poverty strategies; too often, the reali-ties of life with too little money are ignored by those running food and nutrition projects and programmes. Food has been seen as a private, domestic affair; part of 'lifestyle' rather than as a basic entitlement. Solutions to problems are located in change at the individual level, rather than in the social and political decisions which affect structural constraints on everyday life.

The present Government has recognised the basic issues about physical access to shops, and the problems some children face over pro-vision of food through schools. There is an emphasis on partnerships and participation, and calls for 'cross-cutting' policy initiatives. These are exciting possibilities for food and nutrition policy, which has to cut across the traditional sectoral responsibilities: agriculture, retailing, health, education, environment, employment and transport. Box 6.1

sets out a new challenge to Government through *Food Justice,* a campaign to secure duty on Goverment and local authorities, to end food poverty within 15 years. The voluntary and private sectors also have important roles to play. And people themselves, whether rich or poor, have to engage in recognising the challenges and effecting solutions. 'Food poverty' is not only the responsibility of poor families. Food security means all people have access, at all times, to sufficient, safe, acceptable food for a healthy life, and the security of knowing such access is sustainable in the future.

Chapter 5 has shown how much is already happening to improve poor families' food security. This chapter sets out key areas where more could and should be done, and identifies the challenges to all those involved: national and local government, voluntary and private sectors, and those who live on low incomes, as well as their richer neighbours.

BOX 6.1: An end to food poverty – whose responsibility?

There is only so much that local groups, whether or not in partnership with the private sector, can do to ensure all people at all times know they have security of access to sufficient, affordable, safe and appropriate food for a healthy life. They play a part, but the responsibility for doing this has to be government's – centrally and locally. Only they can bring about the structural changes – in income levels, in planning laws, in institutional food provision, in food promotion and retailing – that are needed.

Food Justice: a campaign involving a group of charities and MPs has begun to secure a duty on Government , in conjunction with local authorities, to draw up and implement an action plan to eradicate food poverty within 15 years. A Food Poverty Eradication Bill, previously tabled and to be presented again in the next parliament, would put the responsibility on local authorities to:

- consult with local people, authorities and organisations;
- establish the nature and extent of local problems;
- assess what measures are needed, along with cost and environmental impact;
- draw up local level action plans,

and on central government to:

- draw on local plans and consultations;
- establish the nature and extent of problems;
- assess what central measures are needed;
- draw up a national plan of action – objectives, target dates and to eradicate food poverty within 15 years.[2]

BOX 6.2: **Key areas for reducing food poverty**

- Ensuring people have enough money for food.
- Improving physical and economic access to food.
- Supporting community food initiatives and local projects.
- Protecting mothers and babies.
- Promoting /enabling good food for children.

It complements Sustain's updated report *Food Poverty: What are the Policy Options 2001?* Sustain's report sets out the problems in detail, identifying relevant organisations and responsibilities for policy options listed. What is needed are more pragmatic, practical initiatives that address immediate problems and the development of integrated policy responses at national and local levels, that have reduction in food poverty as a key objective. Box 6.2 lists the key areas which need attention: raising incomes; improving food access; appropriate support for local activities; attention to mothers, babies and children. Mechanisms for bringing these about are discussed in the rest of the chapter.

ENSURING PEOPLE HAVE ENOUGH MONEY FOR FOOD

It is easy to lose sight of the need for an adequate income for food. Many current Government initiatives addressing inequalities in food and health, or poverty and exclusion, focus on area-based initiatives, issues of access and availability, and paid work (Welfare to Work) as solutions. There is no doubt that both child benefit and out-of-work benefits, as well as in-work means-tested benefits (working families' tax credit) have increased since the 1997 election, so that low-income families with dependent children are better off financially. Those who are lone parents, however, are less well off than they might have been had the cuts in lone parents' benefits not been implemented shortly after the election.

The New Labour Government has committed itself to ending child poverty within 20 years, and promises an integrated child credit from 2003, to reconcile current different systems of support for children.[3] The likelihood of child poverty being eliminated by the various proposed means is beyond the scope of this book (CPAG has published an analysis of the Blair Government's record in tackling child and family poverty from 1997, and future prospects[4]). However, Labour's goals of eradicating child poverty imply continual above-inflation increases in financial support for families and children so that significant increases in income are achieved.[5] It is hard to see how this can be managed on current public spending forecasts without an increase in taxation – and Labour has pledged not to increase income tax. Furthermore, recent analysis suggests that the families lifted out of poverty to date have, perhaps inevitably, been those with incomes just below the poverty line and that the mechanisms used depend critically on low unemployment.[6] Families living in long term poverty, and in places where jobs and child care are scarce, or where few jobs pay sufficient to cover child care costs, are least likely to benefit and most likely to remain poor.

It still remains the case that both the structure of work and nature of employment contracts have changed enormously over the last two decades: many jobs are short term, with insecure, piece-work or 'zero hours' contracts.[7] The emphasis on lone parents being required to work has been questioned in terms of parenting responsibilities (which include feeding themselves and their children), and the longer term implications for family income of knock-on eligibility for various in- and out-of-work benefits is not yet clear. The recent *Poverty and Social Exclusion Survey* of Britain gives some indication of the importance of wage levels. This survey showed in some detail the circumstances and experiences of adults and children who were poor, defined in terms of a socially constructed deprivation score. Children who went without two or more items on the list were defined as poor (details of how these definitions were derived are in the survey reports and summaries). Children in households with no workers were nine times more likely to be poor than those in households with two or more full-time workers, but they were 11 times more likely to be poor if they lived in households with only part-time workers.[8]

There has also been a massive increase in inequality of income from earnings over the last two decades. Overall income inequality was higher in 1999/2000 than in 1997 when Labour came to power: the average income of the poorest fifth of households grew at an annual average of 1.4 per cent between 1997 and 2000. During the same period the average income of the richest fifth grew by 2.8 per cent per year.[9] Government strategy towards low pay has been both through in-work benefits (working families' tax credit) and increased child benefit, and through introduction of a national minimum wage. Implementation of this legislation has clearly been important for low income families in paid work: 1.5 million workers' incomes (two-thirds of them women) have been raised.[10] Even so, some 300,000 workers still earn less than the minimum wage, despite Government enforcement systems.[11] The initial rate of the wage was too low to lift workers out of poverty; even with present uprating the rates are likely to be insufficient to meet basic household needs.[12]

There is much survey and observational evidence (cited in Chapters 1 and 2) that in the longer term many families prioritise paying bills and rent above buying food. However, food poverty remains as hidden now as in the past. Debt counsellors, advice workers and the benefits system itself deal with the printed, measured bills for fuel, water, council tax, hire purchase agreements, housing costs and travel to work, and other demands faced by people living with little money. There is no 'food bill' to set alongside such costs; people simply go without, or 'visit' family or friends:

> I was left with nothing on a Friday night. Their father took the giro and left, he left us with nothing, no money. We had enough food for Saturday but I'll tell you Sunday was a long day. The children finished off the bread but that was it. We had to wait until I could get my child benefit before I could go shopping.[13]

Food costs money whether a parent or their children are in or out of work, and food costs for families with dependent children in receipt of income support increases during school holidays, when entitlement to free school meals becomes irrelevant:

> It sounds daft but during the holidays it is much harder making ends meet. The kids are at home all day and all they do is eat. [...] When they are at school they get their dinner, at the holidays they don't and you have to find the money for 10 more meals a week. You notice it when you get to the checkout.[14]

The adequacy of income support and other benefits, and minimum wages to support healthy living has been discussed earlier and elsewhere.[15] Whether poverty is defined in terms of money (absolute or relative amounts) or deprivation, it is still essential to review the sufficiency of income. The principle of budget standards, whether drawn up by professionals or consensual groups, is useful in that it defines a theoretical average income needed to meet basic needs. Recent upratings of the Family Budget Unit *Low Cost but Acceptable* suggest that a couple with two children under 11 years would need to spend at least £62.00 a week, and a lone parent with two children under 11 would need to spend at least £39.25 a week, to buy adequate diets for health, using prices from a major supermarket.[16] It is hard to believe this would be possible for most people on low incomes at present, whether from benefits or low wages, especially where debt repayments are being deducted.[17]

In practice, many people would probably need even more money, because such budget standards usually do not include sensitivity allowances for variations in local costs of rent, fuel, water or food described in Chapter 1. Because incomes from low wages or benefits have been insufficient to meet basic needs, in some instances for many years, many people have got into debt. This is in spite of their having gone without food, or eaten meagre, unsatisfactory diets. The costs of the food budget should play a larger part than at present in establishing repayment rates for fines and debts. In other parts of Europe, budget standards are used to evaluate benefit or minimum wage levels, and in some instances, the costs of meeting adequate food for healthy living are taken into account in setting fines or debt repayments.[18]

People also need money for basic equipment to prepare and cook food. Surveys and 'cook and eat' projects have found many families, particularly younger parents, do not possess simple items such as a sharp knife or chopping board, a mixing bowl, an ovenproof dish, a grater, a wooden spoon, kitchen scales etc, there is also the recognised problem of not having a working cooker (and fridge). Purchase of such basic needs can be difficult when there is little cash to spare, and families are reluctant to take out another social fund loan, or where the local social fund allocation has been used up for the year. The lack of equipment also has implications for health promotion initiatives which encourage poor families to try new foods, or to take part in 'cook and eat' groups.

This issue about how much money people really do need to survive and thrive, and how such levels should be uprated, is itself one which requires attention. Research should not be a one-off inquiry, but part of a continual process of development and testing of methodologies, for use at a national and local level, where specific conditions and circumstances can be taken into account. There is woefully little research on changes over time or between different local situations, and the processes of budgeting and indebtedness. For example, recent longitudinal research on the impact of regeneration to combat social exclusion on low-income households showed clearly how complex assessments need to be to capture the realities of people's experiences of living through such major change. In fact, even though the regeneration initiatives were specifically designed to help reduce deprivation, the evidence showed that the regeneration process itself increased the costs of non-substitutable items (such as rent, council tax and water) so that food expenditure was reduced.[19]

• There is urgent need for more research on levels of income which are sufficient to keep families with children out of poverty. This research must include the voices and experience of those who live in straitened circumstances, as well as those who do not.[20]
• Government and agencies dealing with indebtedness and its financial and legal consequences must recognise that there are severe costs to families when their incomes are insufficient to meet the food budget. These costs are in short-term misery and long-term bad health outcomes.
• Parents on income support with school aged dependants need extra money during school holidays when their children cannot obtain a free school meal.

IMPROVING PHYSICAL AND ECONOMIC ACCESS TO FOOD

For every new Sainsbury Central selling sushi there is a store splitting packs of cigarettes for resale. For each strawberry punnet in a super-market in January or baby corn flown in from Zimbabwe, Peru or Indonesia depending on the season, there is a local shop selling sweets, crisps, and Iron Bru by the gallon.[21]

This book began with a picture of food security: that all people at all times should have physical and economic access to sufficient, safe and acceptable food for an active healthy life, and the security of knowing this access is sustainable in the future (see Chapter 1). Food should be produced in ways that are sustainable, moral and equitable, and people should be able to acquire and share food in ways which do not demean them or their culture.

The Poverty Alliance in Scotland used these ideas as a basis for a series of seminars in their Foodworks Enquiry *From food deserts to food security: an alternative vision*. Participants at the seminars included residents in poor areas, those who lived on low incomes, academics and professionals from local government, retailing, health, social services or education. Many of those taking part could quite easily understand the term 'food desert' – a place where food is either scarce or very limited, where there is no pleasure in shopping, preparing or eating food, and where anxiety about getting enough good food for health dominates what people say and think. They started imagining what it would be like to live in the opposite of a food desert. They conjured up what a 'state of food security' would be like to live in: what food production and distribution systems, public policies and services would need to be in place to distinguish security from a desert, and prevent it happening again.

As a result, their thinking moved from 'a simple focus on income adequacy and household management skills to a realisation that the problems experienced by people living in poverty are only the extreme demonstration of a substantive problem which affects Scotland as a nation'. Their vision included new ways of producing, distributing and retailing food, to the benefit of the many rather than the few, and to sustain vibrant local economies and natural environments. The Poverty Alliance has presented a challenge to the Scottish Parliament: 'to prioritise food security as a national objective and to explore the nature and potential of the food economy in Scotland to contribute to the overall objective for a sustainable, healthy and equitable Scotland'.[22] Food security, which has the potential to benefit the environment, communities and individuals, is a policy challenge for Wales, Northern Ireland and England as well.

This book is not about food production and management in the UK, which have been and remain critical policy issues in the present decade.[23] But we have shown that food access is critical: the shops people can reach, and what food they find in them, at what prices. Here we pick up the threads from Chapters 1 and 3, and summarise current retailing trends and challenges which have potential impact on all society, including poor families.

Food retailing and shopping patterns have changed enormously over the last two decades, and will continue to change in response to consumer demand and demographic shifts:

- people are generally spending more on eating out, and less on food for the home;
- patterns of eating and food purchase are very fragmented compared to the past, both within and between households, and between age groups;
- there are more households, with smaller numbers in each, and consumers expect more and travel more (both for holidays and work, and to shop);
- the population is ageing, more women work outside the home, more people live or want to live outside the inner city (though there are some reverse trends).

Retailers operate in a very competitive environment, and are adapting to new concerns, such as environmental damage and sustainability, and food safety. The growth in supermarket sales of ready meals, home meal replacements and sandwiches, along with hundreds of fresh food lines and massive increases in organic products, is evidence of this responsiveness and determination to survive. Contemporary store management practices have transformed food retailing into a super-efficient, global business, where policies of central storage and 'just in time' store stocking reduces costs and wastage and streamlines processes, so that 'value-for-money' becomes the driving force. There is constant sensitivity to the demands of middle and high income customers for convenience, reassurance and international variety and quality, of which high-quality inner city stores and e-tailing are but two responses.[24]

> For many consumers, the cornucopia of the supermarket and the ritual of the shopping trip have become key sources of satisfaction, security and confidence in a rapidly changing world, where individuality and self-expression have become intimately associated with personal consumption.[25]

The converse of these trends is the increasing dependence on air and road transport to shift food, with knock-on environmental costs, and the deskilling of customers. People now travel further to shop: over three quarters of total mileage for shopping is by car; distances travelled have more than doubled.[26] Poor consumers, of course, are excluded from these trends. People have less confidence in handling food, and the decline in cooking skills is widely documented and lamented. Low income consumers are the most likely to express anxieties about cooking, although there is not much evidence they are actually worse at it than more affluent households. What is clear, is that without skills, people's choice and control are diminished and a dependency culture emerges.[27]

The increasing monetary and spatial exclusion of poor families from this burgeoning economy is described in Chapter 1. The Government initiatives, particularly through the Policy Action Team 13 committee and report (see p22). Yet still much health promotion activity ignores these fundamental issues of access: that food costs more than many poor families can afford; that fresh produce particularly is too heavy to carry home in bulk; that walking or taking buses to shops is difficult with young children or physical disability, is unpleasant (and sometimes unsafe) in many deprived environments, and is often impossible in rural areas.[28]

Public transport which is adequate, cheap or even free, and special needs transport, have important parts to play in enabling people without cars to have access to town centres or out-of-town retail parks, where a range of food and other shops can be found.[29] There are special problems in rural areas, such as the impact of deregulation of buses, and the large distances people have to travel to reach different shops. Inevitably, car ownership or car access is more common.[30] Access to public transport remains an important strategy: the quality and level should be maintained and increased. Some versions of this strategy assume people prefer to shop in the major retailers, with local shops only providing 'top-up' shopping. But in practice, most public transport does not take most people door to door. A family of four, shopping once a week, would have to carry 13kg (about 29lb) of fruit and vegetables, plus the rest of the shopping, from shop to bus stop, and from bus stop home, in order to eat the recommended amounts of fruit and vegetables. This is quite a physical challenge. Secondly, local shops provide an opportunity for people to meet, and can play a vital role in reducing the social isolation of most deprived neighbourhoods.[31] The quality and range of commodities available in many local shops (high fat, high salt, processed foods) needs to be improved, along with better stocking of fresh fruit, vegetables and meat so local shops are good places to shop for healthy food.

There is much anxiety expressed about the drop in physical activity and, it is claimed by some, linked rise in obesity, even among children (although the evidence is not conclusive).[32] Poor children, where rates may be rising fastest, are not necessarily driven to school or the shops by parents in cars, but they also do not play outside as much as they once did, and neither they nor their parents walk or cycle much in physical environments that are increasingly unsafe and unsavoury.[33] The physical and social safety of neighbourhood environments needs a higher focus, and policy activities should not be confined to community based initiatives, valuable though these be. Support for well designed non-motorised carriers for heavy or bulky shopping that can be hired from shops, or easily purchased, should be explored (such as modern trolleys for pushing or attaching to bicycles).

Problems of crime and low retail takings/head of population, plus the poor transport networks, are precisely the reasons given by the major retailers for not siting in areas of material and social deprivation. The recent inquiry into supermarkets found that their practice of selling basic goods below cost price and changing prices according to local competition both damaged small retailers. Smaller local shops, including those run by minority ethnic groups, and discount stores, thus struggle to remain operating for these large but under-serviced communities. They face fiscal and regulatory burdens, and probably suffer unfair competition, with little practical support.[34] In fact, they could play an important role in economic regeneration. Toby Peters, of Community Owned Retailing (see Box 6.3), is a stalwart champion and promoter of ways to achieve such an end. Current regeneration strategies look at attracting more money into deprived areas, but often ignore food problems and needs of both retailers and local communities. A major challenge is retaining within the local area such regeneration funding that is obtained. Some of the poorest estates have no extant businesses – not even a local shop, or only one on the brink of closure. Neighbourhood renewal strategies therefore need to address helping money to circulate more effectively within a community, which could include more positive support for local shops.[35]

> Retailing is currently about the haves and the have-nots being catered for separately. We lament our derelict high streets and the government pursues regeneration policies. But the power of food retailing to cement communities together is being overlooked. 'In any community, the poorer section may not have the spending power to support a good shop, but the community as a whole will have. My argument is that neighbourhoods need viable shops serving the whole community. To achieve that, local shops have to be good enough to keep the people who have a choice, the people who have a car, and can get to the supermarkets. Those shoppers will then help to 'subsidise' the ones who don't have as much to spend.'[36]

Ensuring adequate food access for all requires action at national, as well as at the local level, with concerted effort across government departments. It also needs regional and local authorities to be involved, along with the large retailers and those responsible for core provision in areas of deprivation: small store chains, discount stores and ethnic minority retailers. Currently there is little integration between them and 'joined-up' government policies; there is still a tendency to rely on local food projects and community initiatives to solve food access problems. What is more, local people are themselves seldom involved in the discussions and decision making. Indeed, many people living in deprived communities express considerable scepticism about 'consultation and participation' where retailing and regeneration are concerned. Many have had negative experiences of such activities; they have given time, energy and ideas to consultative processes and the professionals involved, only to find their real needs and desires ignored in the outcomes. There are some positive examples of local authorities or healthy authorities (or both, in Health Action Zones or City Partnerships) trying to work with local people in different ways to improve these consultative processes, and the Government has encouraged such participation. There are also some interesting parallels in consultative work being done about ways of tackling financial exclusion.[38] However, successful examples in relation to food access and local shops provision are not widespread, and many are in early stages.[39]

Key issues in improving food access are:

- **maintaining and improving public transport in areas poorly served by food retailers, along with making walking and cycling safer, more possible and attractive with improved means for carrying food;**
- **investing actively in deprived areas in small businesses such as local shops, by tackling crime, environmental problems, sourcing and management shortfalls, to stimulate circulation of money and maintain the benefits of regeneration in the local economy;**
- **prioritising food access in national and local regeneration and policy frameworks and activities, and establishing responsibility in central government;**
- **involving food retailers themselves in promoting and sustaining access, as well as giving active voice to local consumers and community members.**

SUPPORTING COMMUNITY FOOD INITIATIVES AND LOCAL PROJECTS

The poor are often prodded, probed and studied endlessly, as if they are public property. They often experience such 'study' as yet another subtle form of control over, rather than empowerment in, their lives.[40]

There are four challenges in community food projects:

- the need to reconcile diverse agendas and ownership of projects;
- the need for ongoing rather than start-up funding;
- the future of semi-commercial partnerships;
- the focus on social justice.

BOX 6.3: **Community owned retailing – rescuing local shops from second-class status**

Community owned and run shops can be run for a modest profit but for the benefit of the whole community. An example in Battle, Sussex has as much local produce as possible, with a café on hand to use up unsold fruit and vegetables, and healthy ready-made meals for sale which have been prepared on the premises. Prices are low, though there are pricier treats for those who want to buy them, so people can buy all the basics at supermarket prices.

> This shop is inclusive in practice as well as theory. We have lots of pensioners coming in, people on benefits. Yes, we have tinned beans – but we also have fresh alternatives, at prices people can afford. There's no point in telling people to eat fresh food and support local farmers if there isn't a shop where they can buy the stuff.
> *Toby Peters, proprietor*

Peters argues that a viable community owned shop in deprived areas could work, with fresh produce and ready-prepared food for sale, a café, internet access (so people could bulk order from supermarkets against the shop's credit, and collect deliveries from the shop) and a 'financial services' area with post office facilities and a credit union. Several communities are interested, but none has funding or real backing to put the ideas into effect.[37]

RECONCILING AGENDAS AND OWNERSHIP

In the previous chapter we identified the diverse agendas and concerns which surround community based food projects. Health professionals' project goals may be set nationally by the Department of Health, such as to increase fruit and vegetable consumption to decrease cancer incidence, whereas local people's goals may be to feed their children well so as to stop them going hungry. Local professionals have to inhabit this middle ground, which can be difficult and uncomfortable. They are often not trained or supported to do so, and need creativity within their roles, targets and timetables. They also need other resources to implement activities which often demand multi-disciplinary approaches and skills, and the ability and infrastructure to cross professional boundaries. Such work encompasses a community development approach, which has been shown to be effective in tackling both the social and cultural aspects of healthy eating alongside nutritional issues.[41]

> In terms of community development, I think the problem [...] is that it's very difficult to actually measure what you achieve when other people are achieving it with you. If you say that [...] the community has to own the issue in the first place, and you are actually delivering. It leaves the professional looking for, well, what have I done in that? How do I measure my own success?[42]

The reality for many professionals is that they find themselves trying to implement a hybrid version of community development, one which has the usual time and resources implications but also imposes strict targets and specified outcomes. Organisational and structural frameworks remain inflexible and the resources needed to implement a community development approach are not forthcoming. Funding agencies or those employing professionals can fail to acknowledge the importance of wider social outcomes, and insist on narrower, quantitative health outcome targets being met. Yet public health policy is increasingly about partnerships with local people to reduce health inequalities. While evaluation of 'what works' is essential, the measures of success or failure have to reflect the diversity of interests and goals of all concerned. Community based projects often have to evolve to meet the needs of local people as well as those of funders. The challenge for evaluators is to reconcile these outcomes of interest, to meet community and funders' objectives. Thus, evidence of percentage change in prespecified indicators may be appropriate for monitoring or evaluation, but must have a negotiated value alongside process indicators of change, or less tangible outcomes such as an increase in confidence, feelings of wellbeing and empowerment.

Shared ownership of projects between professionals and communities is a critical factor in their success, as is recognising the time and effort needed by both. Local people have to be seen as part of the solution, as well as part of the problem; as equal partners with professionals, with expertise and experience to contribute.[43] From the planning stage onwards, when problems, needs and wants are being identified and project possibilities being considered, local people must be involved, not as objects of consultation but as true, participative owners of the processes involved.[44] Then their perceptions of the problems, knowledge and experience of which projects will win community support and ideas for wider solutions and links with professionals and agencies, will be incorporated into the projects. Facilitating community full participation and ownership are critical to projects' success and sustainability. The implications for policy are once again related to the need for adequate resourcing, realistic expectations and time frames.

Both volunteers and professionals alike often need to learn new ways of working to make local food projects effective, as well as training in, and recognition of, new skills. Public health personnel and those from a community development background each need to develop capacities to operate in different professional frameworks or approaches. They often also need to learn new information and technical skills. Project volunteers may also need new technical and personal skills. All will need supportive environments to foster both career development and confidence to cross disciplinary and professional boundaries.

> I mean, I've got women I work with just now […] that woman's secured a quarter of a million pound from the lottery […] and you get social workers coming in and attempting to tell her what to do […] She's confident enough now to say 'go away' in no uncertain terms, but it's about recognising people and their value.[45]

ONGOING FUNDING

Many projects spend huge amounts of time and energy chasing funding, particularly for on going costs. Monies are fairly readily available for start-up and innovation; but support for running costs is much more difficult to find; the guidelines of many funding bodies specifically exclude them. As a result, projects have constantly to reinvent themselves to qualify again for set-up funding. Sometimes this is a creative activity as it enables projects to evolve into new activities or ways of working. However, for many it is simply a diversion and a continual source of anxiety. Access to on going funding (or becoming self-sufficient, which is not common and is difficult to maintain) is crucial to project sustainability. If funding is short-term or withdrawn, or if a project fails to secure follow-on funds, there are severe demands placed on professionals and volunteers. These are common findings for many community based activities: food projects are no different. The challenge for funders is to find a way to reward success (to continue some level of funding) rather than penalising it (withdrawing or reducing funding) while enabling new projects to get off the ground.

Food projects can also be supported through informal means, through hidden subsidies: tangibles such as free access to buildings (or very low rents) and loan of vehicles and equipment, or support and time from volunteers and others. These should be facilitated and increased wherever possible.

SEMI-COMMERCIAL PARTNERSHIPS

The hope is sometimes expressed that projects will become self-financing: will raise sufficient revenue internally through sales, so as to reduce the dependence on external support. There is of course the intrinsic problem that if it had been possible to maintain a viable commercial enterprise in the area (for instance, a local café serving healthy food choices, or small fresh produce shop) the community initiative would not have been needed. The only reason food is cheaper in community initiatives (cafés, co-ops, etc) is that voluntary labour is being used and there are hidden subsidies of low rents/free premises/loans of (insured) vehicles, and so forth. However, some food co-ops and community cafes have been running for ten years or more, and there are examples of partnerships with local authorities or wholesalers which have reduced the dependence on external funding. More work needs to be done exploring these possibilities, and examining the costs and benefits to either side.

Community food projects are sometimes linked to micro-finance initiatives, such as credit unions, both in terms of structures and aims of anti-poverty and anti-social exclusion, and in terms of location (credit unions are often found in the same building as a food co-op or community café, and open at the same time). Credit unions, like community food projects, provide a service that mainstream private sector institutions (in this instance, high street banks) refuse to engage in, and they empower and equip low income communities to address their own problems, owning their own solutions and gaining useful skills and confidence at the same time.[46] There is some concern that the proposed new 'universal bank' in post offices could undermine the viability of credit unions by targeting the same client groups.

Recent research on micro-finance initiatives/credit unions in Central America showed they had similar objectives to British credit unions (and community food projects) and were similarly being pushed towards semi-commercialisation. They are perhaps further along the line than here; many operated on the boundaries between small, struggling local initiatives and networked, larger institutionalised systems, sometimes within a semi-commercial framework. The research showed that this trend towards institutionalisation tends to lead to 'cherry-picking' both the best clients and services provided, which in turn excluded the poorest either actively or through self-selection, and reduced the range of service options on offer.[47]

This research with credit unions in developing countries has some parallels with community food projects, though there has been little longitudinal research on the latter. The Joseph Rowntree Foundation funded study of food projects found that:

- some had gone through several cycles of reinvention to chase funding. Such switching of activities was driven by funding or professionals' needs rather than those of the community;
- some, almost by default, had only retained as members/customers those who were able to give time (eg, to attend a 'cook and eat' class) or who could plan sufficiently ahead (eg, to place orders with a food co-op, knowing they would have the money to pay for a week's vegetables) – ie, they excluded the poorest;
- some had tried a range of activities to address food poverty, and had had to settle for 'what worked', rather than what met their original objectives. Often they chose activities for pragmatic reasons, such as the activities fitting the job description of the professional involved, or being deemed appropriate for the project setting;
- some had become very successful in terms of lists of members or turnover, in terms of a voluntary driven organisation, and were even moving across boundaries into semi-commercial activities, yet were in fact probably non-viable financially, or simply too small, in comparison with actual small commercial businesses with whom they might compete for customers, or funding.

There are initiatives towards creative sourcing for food co-ops and breakfast clubs, for instance, with networking for wholesale and local schools as regular outlets. These are good moves, and will help in certain parts of the country. However, there is also, conversely, the issue of whether community food projects thus resourced will damage such small local commercial operations as do remain in poor communities, unless they work together with them. The commercial wholesale market for fruit and vegetables has struggled to survive the hegemony of the big retailers over the last decade, and people running small green-grocers cannot access the same networks of support from local authorities or funding agencies such as the National Lottery, because they are not running 'community' initiatives. Yet their turnover, even in a deprived area, can outrank that of a food co-op, and they have more commercially at stake than a volunteer-run enterprise, so may be less prepared to take risks. Partnerships between community food projects and local small businesses are easily encouraged on paper but they have proved hard to realise in practice, and need creative support.

SOCIAL JUSTICE

Community food projects are potentially powerful and empowering activities, providing common ground for local people and professionals to work together in innovative ways. They enable people to have better access to healthy food, gain confidence and skills and to improve food intakes and wellbeing. However, they also raise critical issues of social justice.

The first is whether those who are 'poor', and who live in areas where many others are poor, should have to live differently, or expect a different solution, from those who are poor but do not live in poor areas, or from the rest of the population. Why should such citizens not be able to shop for food like everyone else? Why should the solution to their problems have to be self-help, rather than the mix of commercial and state supported provision found in places where income levels are more mixed, or higher? There is not yet a requirement imposed on those who live in areas where water is expensive and/or difficult to provide, that they have to organise a chain of buckets to a community standpipe. Why is that then a solution for food? No one expects those who are richer to get up at 4.30 in the morning to buy vegetables for 45 families for a week, and then spend all morning weighing and bagging them up, unpaid. Why should poor families have to do it every week in a food co-op? There is nothing wrong with volunteering; it is actively encouraged by the Government. Taking part in community activities and working with neighbours are good for people: those who do so have better health, are more positive and happier, and live longer.[48] The fundamental issues are about choice: to do these things because you want to do them and are supported in doing them, not because it is the only way to feed your family.

Secondly, solutions to tackle food poverty have to avoid expecting people on low incomes, who may lead very difficult, fractured lives, being asked to succeed where professionals and policy makers have failed. What is worse, they are often asked to tackle these issues with fewer resources, less support and often within a shorter time-frame, than professionals would be expected to do. Of course involving local people is vital to the success of food initiatives as part of an anti-food poverty strategy, but it must be as a *part*, not the only strategy, and local people have to be involved in genuine partnership where they are asked to achieve realistic tasks with sufficient financial and other support.

Community food projects need:

● **genuine partnership between local people and professionals; community ownership; realistic, flexible time-frames and goals;**
● **proper resourcing, especially ongoing funding for running costs, rather than focus on start-up; adequate back-up and support;**
● **realism about semi-commercial partnerships and potential achievements;**
● **social justice: engagement in structural change and support for genuine choice.**

PROTECTING MOTHERS AND BABIES

There is no doubt that the future health of any nation depends on the health of its children, which in turn depends on the health of their mothers. We have described how important a mother's own nutritional and health history is for the wellbeing of her present and future babies. Yet there are still widespread health inequalities among women of childbearing age and among young children. The Government is consulting on work to tackle health inequalities with a cross-cutting spending review to help prioritise actions.[49] One of the ten taskforces being created to drive forward implementation of the *NHS Plan* is charged with child health and reducing inequalities. One of the two national health inequalities targets announced in February 2001 is to reduce the gap in infant mortality (deaths in children under one year old) between manual groups and the whole population, by at least 10 per cent by 2010. The main means of achieving this seems to be through Sure Start programmes, extended to include pregnant women and their partners, from conception rather than birth. However, significant opportunities to focus systematically on an evidence based national public health strategy to improve the long term health of the child bearing population and their children, are being missed. For example, the timing and nature of reform of the welfare foods scheme is not mentioned in any current health documents other than saying it will be done by 2004 and will *'use resources more effectively to ensure children in poverty have access to a healthy diet'*.[50]

A consultative conference organised by the Maternity Alliance produced a set of key recommendations.[51] They included increased

flexibility within the welfare foods scheme, in terms of who partici-
pates, what foods are covered and appropriateness of nutrients delivered
and the levels. Participants particularly stressed that the scheme should
be seen and promoted as a public health measure to improve the health
of children and the childbearing population, rather than as a partial
safety net for nutritionally vulnerable pregnant women and babies.
There was a strong call to 'rebrand' the scheme to reflect the central
health concern rather than as a welfare response, and that a cross-
departmental Maternal and Child Health Taskforce be established to
formulate and promote such a strategy.

The Maternity Alliance, among others, has produced a comprehensive set of proposals to address the public health needs of women of
childbearing age and their children, many of which are food related.[52]
We draw on their proposals here. Firstly, in relation to pregnancy: the
current health inequalities agenda needs targets for improvements in
reproductive health. Currently there are none, except for reducing
teenage pregnancy. Secondly, young women's nutritional status is more
likely to be poor if they are from a low social class or deprived area.
Benefit rates for pregnant women should be increased. They have not
changed over the last few years in line with other benefits, and women
depending on income support or jobseeker's allowance cannot afford a
healthy diet. This is particularly the case for pregnant women under 25
years old, who still receive a reduced rate. Even worse, some pregnant
women under 20 years old are not entitled to any benefit or welfare
foods until the last 11 weeks of pregnancy. Those who do qualify for
benefit get a lower rate than older women. Since the health of teenage
mothers is often compromised by poor nutrition, and teenagers are 25
per cent more likely than average to deliver a low birthweight baby, their
benefits should be set at a level which is more appropriate for a healthy
pregnancy diet. The age discrimination in benefits should be ended,
certainly for pregnant women, despite any notional potential for benefit
abuse. Thirdly, unsupported pregnant teenagers should be provided with
access to benefits and welfare foods and their health and food needs
should be targeted by teenage pregnancy co-ordinators and Sure Start
Plus (which currently focuses on prevention and support). Finally, there
are over 10,000 officially homeless pregnant women in temporary
accommodation, and probably many more unofficially homeless living
with friends or relatives, or sleeping rough. Such women particularly
need financial and other practical and emotional support.

In terms of support for parents with very young children, the problems facing those who are homeless (usually mothers but sometimes

fathers as well) and their children are severe. More than 50,000 homeless households include young children. Minimum environmental standards should be enforced for temporary hostels, including provision of appropriate kitchen and food storage facilities. Vulnerable ex-homeless new mothers particularly need help and support, not least over feeding themselves, their babies and their young children.[53] All mothers in Britain need more practical and material support to begin and maintain breastfeeding, but this is especially the case for mothers living in deprived areas or on low incomes. The documents on inequalities in health hardly mention practical breastfeeding initiatives, yet poorer mothers are the least likely to initiate or continue breastfeeding. Poorer mothers in low paid jobs are less likely to have access to time and space to breastfeed or express their milk. More investment should be made in peer support programmes aimed at disadvantaged women. The conflicting messages from the welfare foods scheme need to be clarified; currently the scheme contributes to normalising bottle feeding among women on means-tested benefits and discourages breastfeeding by providing vouchers for formula feeds. The Maternity Alliance consultation report discusses alternative models of improving the system.[54]

Research in the US (see Box 6.4), Canada and in developing countries has shown that small investments in maternal and early childhood nutrition have large potential impact in health and wellbeing throughout childhood and through to adulthood.[55] There needs to be much more research in Britain on the implications of dietary regimes and the effects of restrictions on diet, during and before pregnancy, in terms of birthweight, child development, and other outcomes. Feeding teenagers a better diet is not only important for their own health; if they are female, it is critical for the health of their future children.

Mothers (and babies) need:

- **access to sufficient money to eat healthily during pregnancy, especially if they are on benefits, and/or under 20 years old;**
- **speedy resolution of the welfare food scheme review;**
- **better support and facilities for homeless pregnant women and/or their babies;**
- **practical breastfeeding support, including strengthening of rights for working women to have time and space to breastfeed.**

ENABLING CHILDREN TO OBTAIN GOOD FOOD

> The Scottish Executive should consider how to switch off the diet of junk food advertising that children are fed while watching TV […] and clamp down on what is euphemistically called 'in-school marketing' where manufacturers of crisps and fizzy drinks can promote their products in cash-strapped schools by offering books and sports equipment in return for spent wrappers.[56]

> I explained to my eldest son that we could claim free school meals. If you could have seen the look of horror on his face you would understand why I don't claim them.[57]

A policy briefing on Healthy Food Policy held by the Scottish Council Foundation in February 2000, argued there were compelling reasons for putting children and families at the heart of healthy food policy.[58] Such a focus would engender a wide commitment to bringing about change in the many areas/agencies/sectors needed to ensure food security. It would also improve and protect the prospects of the next generation of adults. The present health and wellbeing of children is compromised through inadequate diets and miserable experiences of eating; as we describe above, the possibilities that the present generation of girls will be healthy mothers, able to bear healthy babies who in turn grow into healthy adults, is also at risk.

There are two key areas:

- advertising and promotion of food to children;
- food and nutrition in schools: provision and teaching.

Many parents, and particularly those on low incomes, say they want to know more about what is in the food their children eat. One activity of the Food Standards Agency has been to investigate what consumers want on food labels and to improve the clarity and reliability of the information presented.[59] This work needs encouragement; products are still being marketed in misleading ways, particularly high-profit branded goods, and similar foods with lower salt, sugar and fat are seldom as heavily promoted.[60] But these initiatives will only have limited success without changes in the ways foods are marketed to children.

Food advertising and promotion is big business, particularly for processed products. For instance, in 1992, £523 million was spent on TV promotion of food and soft drinks on TV, whereas only £4.5 million was spent promoting fresh fruit and vegetables. Promotion and

---

BOX 6.4: US Special Supplemental Nutrition Program for Women Infants and Children (WIC)

The WIC program has been running in the United States since the early 1970s. WIC is administered at Federal level by the Food and Nutrition Service of the Department of Agriculture; grants are made to states through Departments of Health. State agencies receive funding applications from local private or public health service providers, who are the ultimate implementers of the programme.

WIC provides:
• supplementary foods;
• nutrition education/counselling to high-risk pregnant and lactating women, infants and children under 5 years old (eligibility depends on income and health status).

Depending on the state, women may receive:
• a 'nutritious food parcel';
• vouchers for specific foods, exchangeable in supermarkets or identified stores;
• coupons for authorised farmers' markets.

WIC participation may also open the door for referrals to other health and social care services (such as drug user units or anti-smoking therapy). Some see this as a useful means of enabling disadvantaged women to make desired changes in their lives; others see it as paternalistic and demoralising.

Evaluation of WIC participation has been widely carried out and documented. A much quoted finding is that participants had lower Medicaid costs for themselves and for treatment for underweight and/or premature babies and infants than non-participants (state savings of $1.77-$3.13 for each $1 spent on prenatal WIC benefits). WIC has political support from the Right and the Left, for a variety of reasons, and from health professionals and farmers alike. In 1999, WIC cost US$3.9 billion; an average of 7.3 million received WIC benefits each month. For further information see: http://www.ers.usda.gov/briefing/foodnutritionassistance/wic

---

advertising is not only confined to TV; there is widespread sponsorship by food and drink manufacturers and retailers in sport, education, clubs, computer games, and licensing of cartoon characters to promote particular goods. Children are a particularly key target for promotion of sweets, snacks, fast foods and sweetened breakfast cereals. More than 80 per cent of the advertisements on children's TV are for these products.[61]

Policy makers at national and local levels need to engage with food manufacturers and retailers to change the way incentives are used. Ideas from the Scottish healthy food policy meeting included tokens towards computer games, CDs, sporting events that could be collected with purchases of fruits, fresh vegetables, low fat or low salt items, for example. The principle could be extended to fast food chains (perhaps promoting the growth of 'healthy fast foods').[62] In Sweden, the content and timing of TV advertising for food and other children's products is strictly regulated. There is a strong case for reviewing in Britain where the boundaries of marketing of consumer goods to children, particularly for food, should lie. These issues apply to all children, but the benefits to poor children would be particularly strong, given the case set out above. A recent report from Sustain sets out recommendations to the Food Standards Agency (FSA), the Independent Television Commission (ITC) and to the food industry – see Box 6.5.[63]

In relation to food in schools, the key issues are:

- free school meals: access, quality and uptake;
- schools' food: quality and uptake.

Parents are often unaware of entitlement to free school meals, or are deterred from applying because they do not know how the system works.[64] Schools, local education authorities and benefit offices need to ensure parents know their eligibility and how to apply. CPAG, among others, is campaigning to extend the entitlement to free school meals to all families receiving tax credits in England and Wales. Although there is a notional amount included in working families' tax credit for school meals, the level of the benefit is itself insufficient to meet everyday needs, and any compensatory amount is subsumed into meeting daily living costs.[65] Furthermore, the taper system means that the value of the compensation is reduced by up to 85 per cent for families receiving housing benefit and council tax benefit.[66]

Take-up of free school meals which currently go to children of parents claiming income support needs to be addressed. As discussed in Chapter 2, parents and their children are afraid of the stigma and embarrassment of being labeled 'different'. The use of free tickets or tokens for meal payments, or lists of free meal recipients, or systems which demarcate free meal recipients, should be phased out as soon as possible. Also, schools where no hot service is provided, who give pupils free packed lunches, should avoid distinctive packaging for the free meal.[67] Schools should reassure parents their children will not be identified or identifiable as recipients of free meals. The Scottish bill to provide free and nutritious meals to all pupils has implications for the rest of Britain and its progress should be monitored.

BOX 6.5: Summary of recommendations on TV food advertising to children

The FSA should:

- advise Government on statutory controls rather than a voluntary code of practice on promotion of foods to children;
- facilitate UK wide and/or European legislation to protect children from excessive or unfair advertising, marketing and promotional activities;
- support more effective promotion of fruit and vegetables.

The ITC should review its Code of Advertising Standards and Practice to:

- prohibit advertising or promotion of unhealthy foods during children's peak viewing time;
- give greater protection to younger children who may be more easily misled;
- bring within its scope the effect of advertising as a whole rather than individual adverts;
- enforce the Code effectively.

The industries (food, advertising, media) should:

- show greater responsibility towards children's nutrition, eradicating unhealthy foods advertising from children's TV;
- ensure marketing strategies and promotional activities do not exploit children's age or vulnerabilities.

Source: Sustain, *TV Dinners*, Sustain 2001

Many schools with cafeteria systems are adopting cashless tills which use smart cards. Using cards to pay for meals means those who received a free meal cannot be identified by other pupils or by canteen staff (except anyone operating a till). There are additional potential nutritional/health benefits, in that some schools have enabled those choosing a 'healthy' meal to register rewards on the card (such as swimming pool access). Smart cards are used for recording attendance, security, and access to libraries and other facilities, as well as for paying for school food. The technology is rapidly becoming cheaper and more accessible, and the multi-purpose usage makes it more plausible for schools to afford it. It should be widely adopted and supported.

Since nearly one in three children do not go home to a cooked meal, the school meal must be a guaranteed source of nutritional quality. The enforcement of the minimal nutritional standards is essential, and can only be achieved at a reasonable minimal cost allowance. This should currently be at about £1.50 a head for secondary pupils and about £1.20-£1.30 a head for primary schools, to allow for two courses and a drink.[68] These minimum cost standards must be applied to the free school meal, which then forms the basis for the rest of the meal delivery. Such minimun cost standards must apply to packed lunch quality as well as hot food. In many schools, the free meal ticket does not currently cover the cost of sufficient food to fill the child up, healthily, or to include a drink.[69] Schools should check that the free meal ticket or allowance keeps pace with prices and permits pupils to make healthy choices. Maintaining the quality of free school meals at designated cost not only ensures that children who particularly need it are likely to get the essential nutritional boost, but is also less likely to alienate children from eating school meals at all, free or otherwise. What is more, if schools supply the free school meal well, then the rest of the service is also likely to be a reasonable standard: all children benefit. If the Government, local education authorities and schools seriously want to address problems of take-up of free school meals, they must put in place strategies to ensure the quality of the food and the environment in which it is delivered. Monitoring food quality and cost in relation to current school nutritional guidelines and accountability to parents must be part of these strategies.

Breakfast clubs, which provide pre-school care plus the provision of food, are a more recent feature of school life, particularly in primary schools. Such clubs are becoming increasingly common throughout the country although at present their distribution is patchy.[70] Breakfast clubs serve a variety of functions. The first is to meet the needs of children who may arrive at school in the morning without having eaten. The second is to serve the needs of parents who leave for work early and therefore require child care provision. Schools that run such clubs also identify a third function that is linked to the behaviour of pupils: the clubs are perceived as calming children down before school begins.[71]

Although the Government supports such initiatives there is little sustainable financial support for either establishing or running breakfast clubs. However, money for setting up and supporting them is essential even when parents contribute towards the cost of provision. Support for providing food at breakfast clubs, especially for those children entitled to free school meals, could form part of Health Action Zone or Education Action Zone initiatives. Schools cannot provide such support on their own; this is especially true in deprived areas where the majority of children are living in poverty.

The cost of a basic breakfast that includes cereal, toast and a drink (juice or milk) is currently estimated to be about 35 pence, although the prices currently charged vary.[72] In one school, in a typical of an area of London, parents pay £1 for a breakfast club that runs from 8.00 am to 8.50 am. In this school up to 100 children are on the register, although generally only about 35 are present at any one session.[73] Observations on this breakfast club provide insights into food provision:

> Breakfast club: toast – lots! and cereals. 'Healthy' cereals were tried but children were not interested so they now have frosted and chocolate types. Milk and orange juice with no added sugar are available.

It would be fair to say that at present breakfast clubs are run principally for working parents. The food access issues for children whose parents are out of work, and therefore cannot afford breakfast club charges need to be separate from 'childminding' provision for working parents, some of whom may not earn enough to pay the charges either. Poorer children would certainly benefit from food served before and/or after school. One solution is for the cost of food for breakfast to be subsidised in the same way as school lunches. Schools cannot work on their own to address this issue. Certainly it should not be the responsibility of head teachers to keep cereals for children who arrive in school hungry, something that happens currently in some primary schools in London.[74]

After school provision (eg, homework clubs) is similar to breakfast clubs in being a localised response to particular needs. After school provision is again often designed to meet the needs of working parents whose children would otherwise have to go home, without super-vision, to an empty house or flat. Many of these 'clubs' operate in schools or in adventure playgrounds or halls close to schools. Like breakfast clubs, the funding of after school provision, as well as their rationale, varies. The majority of such clubs make a daily charge (in one area of London £3 was the norm for clubs that ran from 3.15 pm until 6.00 pm during 1999/2000), not least to cover food provision. This is generally in the form of a snack, although hot food may also be provided and sometimes children are involved in the preparation. The food provided by one club was:

> toast – lots; beans on toast; spaghetti on toast; chicken hot dogs. Fruit is also available although the person responsible thought she should

serve more. She finds that when the fruit is cut up or sectioned the children fight over it but if served whole they tend to leave it alone. Sometimes they are served food made by classes during a cookery lesson.[75]

One way forward for children whose parents could not afford to pay would be to extend the provision of food after school, providing food free to those children who are entitled to free school meals. Such support could come from Health Action Zone or Education Action Zone resources. However, such provision will only be of benefit if the food provided is of sufficient quality, variety and amount. For children who attend the breakfast club, eat a school meal in the middle of the day and then attend an after school club, the food they eat in school may be the only food they consume during weekdays. Thus schools play a vital role in food access for some pupils. For these children it is essential that there is monitoring of food provision and food intakes to ensure that such children are eating a varied and balanced diet that conforms to current guidelines. The guidelines for nutritional standards for school meals should be extended to cover provision before and after school, and during holiday clubs, where these are run. The Caroline Walker Trust has recently produced guidelines for food and drink provided by carers of children in residential homes and foster care, which may be relevent here.[76]

Breakfast and homework clubs need access to ongoing funding and support for volunteer efforts, particularly for schools in deprived areas. There are guidelines for setting up and running such initiatives, and sources of support.[77] The healthy school initiative requires a 'whole school approach' to food policy throughout the curriculum and the school day. This should include what is served in breakfast and homework clubs, what is available from tuck shops, rules about food brought in to school, and policy on vending machines. Schools are vulnerable to sponsorship deals from firms and retailers, for vending machines, equipment and teaching materials. Again, it may be difficult for schools in deprived areas to avoid taking inappropriate sponsorship money, especially where there are few active parent teacher associations (PTAs) experienced at raising extra resources for the school. One particularly critical area is in vending machines dispensing sweets, high fat snacks, and fizzy drinks; these are often placed in schools in return for much needed sponsorship money. These are hard to resist from either a financial or popularity perspective. In terms of alternatives, there have been some successful initiatives with fruit tuck shops at primary levels,[78] and the National School Fruit Initiative, currently only aimed at children aged 4 6 years old, may create a demand which supports schools in following suit for older children. Many children only drink fizzy drinks because their schools do not have adequate (or any) drinking water facilities. (Indeed, some children do not drink during the day because school toilet facilities are so unpleasant.) There is currently only non-regulatory guidance to schools about drinking water provision. There should be a more rigorous requirement for access to good quality water, clean toilets with soap and hand towels for washing, and this should be monitored under Ofsted inspection.

Enabling children to obtain good food needs:

- **guidelines, legislation and monitoring of food advertising and promotion to children, to empower them to make appropriate, mature choices about food;**
- **improved entitlement and access to free school meals to all recipients of tax credits; ultimately, possibly, to all children;**
- **protection of school budgets for food provision;**
- **improved quality of school meals, whether free or purchased, and monitoring of such quality both by school inspection and by parents;**
- **support for the whole school approach to food policy, in relation to food provision, vending machines, sponsorship deals, and drinking water.**

SUMMARY

This chapter has summarised in some detail the components of the key strategies to improve food security for poor families. We have reviewed five areas:

- ensuring people have enough money for food;
- improving physical and economic access to food;
- supporting community food initiatives and local projects;
- protecting mothers and babies;
- promoting and enabling good food for children.

Food security for all and an end to food poverty is not about charity or hand-outs. It is about rights and responsibilities. In 1936, John Boyd Orr published the results of a survey of adequacy of diet in relation to income. He showed that the degree of adequacy for health increased as income rose, as did the state of health: 'as income increases, disease and death-rate decrease, children grow more quickly, adult stature is greater and general health and physique improve.' He went on, 'If these findings be accepted... they raise important economic and political problems...[..] one of the main difficulties in dealing with these problems is that they are not within the sphere of any single Department of State.'[79] More than 60 years later we are still facing the same problems: that there are people in Britain whose health and wellbeing are seriously constrained by the diet they are forced to eat, because of lack of money for food, because they cannot get to decent shops, because they lack confidence or scope to try new foods or because their children are not offered reasonable, quality food for health at school. This problem, which is shameful in one of the richest countries in the world, requires concerted, focused and serious effort by Government, at central and local levels, across sectors and organisations, and in partnership with the private and voluntary sectors in different spheres. Then food security can be within the grasp of all.

NOTES

1 D Killeen, 'Food security: a challenge for Scotland', in: J McCormick (ed), *Healthy Food Policy: On Scotland's menu?*, Scottish Council Foundation with the Joseph Rowntree Foundation, 2000

2 For further information contact Ron Bailey, 62 Bargery Road, London SE6 2LW, email ron-bailey@bargery-rd.fsnet.co.uk

3 M Barnes and G Fimister, 'Children's benefits and credits: is an integrated child credit the answer?' in: G Fimister (ed), *An End in Sight? Tackling child poverty in the UK*, CPAG, 2001

4 G Fimister (ed) *An end in sight? Tackling child poverty in the UK* – see note 3

5 Institute of Fiscal Studies, Election Briefing note no 9, 2001

6 D Piachaud and H Sutherland, *How Effective is the British Government's Attempt to Reduce Child Poverty?*, CASE Paper 38, LSE/STICERD, 2000

7 'Zero hour' contracts refers to contracts where workers have to be available for work if needed, at very short notice, but are only paid (usually low wages) if they actually work. Such contracts (in factory or retail, for instance) are often taken by women with dependent children, who may have to find child care at equally short notice.

8 D Gordon, L Adelman, K Ashworth, J Bradshaw, R Levitas, S Middleton, C Pantazis, D Patsios, S Payne, P Townsend and J Williams, *Poverty and Social Exclusion in Britain*, Joseph Rowntree Foundation, 2000

9 Institute of Fiscal Studies, 2001, *The Structure of Welfare*, Election 2001

Briefing note no.11; CPAG, *Campaigns Newsletter* no 16, 2001

10 R Exell, 'Employment and poverty', in G Fimister (ed), *An End in Sight? Tackling child poverty in the UK*, CPAG, 2001

11 L Smith, 'The case for a decent minimum wage', *Poverty* Winter 2001, p3

12 J Morris, A J M Donkin, D Wonderling, P Wilkinson and E Dowler, 'The minimum price of good health', *The New Review* (published by the Low Pay Unit), Mar/Apr 2001, pp11-13; J Morris et al, 'A minimum income for healthy living', *Journal of Epidemiology and Community Health*, 54, 2000, pp885-889

13 Quoted in B Dobson, K Kellard with D Talbot, *A Recipe for Success? An Evaluation of a Community Food Project*, University of Loughborough: Centre for Research in Social Policy, 2000, p 52.

14 See note 13

15 S Leather, *The Making of Modern Malnutrition: An overview of food poverty in the UK*, The Caroline Walker Trust, 1996; E Dowler and C Calvert, 'Budgeting for food on state benefits: poor lone parents in the United Kingdom', in: B Köhler, E Feichtinger, E Barlösius and E Dowler (eds), *Poverty and Food in Welfare Societies*, Sigma Edition, 1997, pp 307-315; J Morris, A J M Donkin, D Wonderling, P Wilkinson and E Dowler, 'A minimum income for healthy living', *Journal of Epidemiology and Community Health*, 54, 2000, pp885-889.

16 N Oldfield, Family Budget Unit, personal communication, August 2001.

17 Nearly 750,000 lone parent families had deductions from income support and/or JSA in 1999, half of which were repayments of social fund loans – ie, for the cost of purchasing basic household items; DSS Analytical Division 1.

18 National Consumer Council (ed), *Budgeting for Food on Benefits: Budget studies and their application in Europe*, National Consumer Council, 1995

19 P Ambrose and D MacDonald, *For Richer, For Poorer? Counting the costs of regeneration in Stepney*, Health and Social Policy Research Centre, University of Brighton, 2001

20 Consensual budget standards research has found that groups of parents living on different levels of income work better than groups differentiated into those on high and low incomes – S Middleton, personal communication.

21 L Sparks, 'Issues in food retailing in Scotland', in: J. McCormick (ed), *Healthy Food Policy: On Scotland's menu?*, Scottish Council Foundation with the Joseph Rowntree Foundation, 2000, p33.

22 D Killeen, *Food Security: A challenge for Scotland*, The Poverty Alliance, 162 Buchanan Street, Glasgow G1 2LL.

23 See G Harvey, 1998, *The Killing of the Countryside*, London: Vintage; J Humphreys, *The Food Question, The Great Food Gamble*, Hodder and Stoughton, 2001

24 L Sparks, 'Issues in food retailing in Scotland', in: J McCormick (ed), *Healthy Food Policy: On Scotland's menu?*, Scottish Council Foundation with

the Joseph Rowntree Foundation, 2000, p32-45.

25 M Harrison and T Lang, 'Running on empty', *Demos Collection,* 12, 1997, pp25-27

26 T Lang and M Caraher, 'Access to healthy foods: part II. Food poverty and shopping deserts: what are the implications for health promotion policy and practice?' *Health Education Journal,* 57, 1998, pp202-211

27 M Caraher and T Lang, 'Can't cook, won't cook: a review of cooking skills and their relevance to health promotion', *International Journal of Health Promotion and Education,* 37, 3, 1999, pp89-100

28 M Caraher, P Dixon, T Lang and R Carr-Hill, 'Access to healthy foods: part 1. Barriers to accessing healthy foods: differentials by gender, social class, income and mode of transport', *Health Education Journal,* 57, 1998, pp191-201; T Lang and M Caraher, 'Access to healthy foods: part II. Food poverty and shopping deserts: what are the implications for health promotion policy and practice?' *Health Education Journal,* 57, 1998, pp202-211

29 TRaC, 2000, Social Exclusion and the Provision and Availability of Public Transport, TraC, University of North London for the Department of the Environment, Transport and the Regions (see: www.mobility-unit.dtlr. gov.uk/socialex2/04.htm accessed August 2001)

30 M Harrison, C Hitchman, I Christie and T Lang, *Running on Empty,* Demos, forthcoming (2001)

31 See work by David Rex , Food Policy Advisor, Sandwell Health Authority; E Dowler, D Rex, A Blair, A Donkin and C Grundy, *Mapping Access to Healthy Food in Sandwell,* Report to the Sandwell Health Action Zone, 2001

32 M B E Livingstone, 'Childhood obesity in Europe: a growing concern', *Public Health Nutrition,* 4, 1A, 2001, pp109-116

33 A Coggins, D Swanston and H Crombie, *Physical Activity and Inequalities: A briefing paper,* Health Education Authority, 1999.

34 New Policy Institute, *Food Access: Whose responsibility?,* New Policy Institute, 2000

35 B Ward in J Seymour, (ed) *Poverty in Plenty: a Human development Report for the UK,* London: Earthscan, 2000; Sandwell report in note 31.

36 Toby Peters, quoted in interview by Lindy Sharpe, *Let Us Eat Cake!,* Newsletter of the Food Poverty Network, Sustain, issue 20, Spring 2001, p12

37 See note 36

38 S Collard, E Kempson and C Whyley, *Tackling Financial Exclusion: An area based approach,* The Policy Press for the Joseph Rowntree Foundation, 2001

39 See the Community Mapping work being promoted and supported by Sustain, the Alliance for Food and Farming; work by Sandwell Health Action Zone, contact David Rex, Sandwell Health Authority; Devon County Council, contact Ian Hutchcroft, Devon Rural Recovery Unit.

40 R Labonté, 'Health promotion in the near future: remembrances of activism past', *Health Education Journal,* 58, pp365-77, quoted in B Dobson, K Kellard with D Talbot, *A Recipe for Success? An Evaluation of a Community Food Project,*

University of Loughborough: Centre for Research in Social Policy, 2000, p77
41 B Dobson, K Kellard with D Talbot, *A Recipe for Success? An Evaluation of a Community Food Project*, University of Loughborough: Centre for Research in Social Policy, 2000
42 Health promotion worker in food co-op, quoted in P McGlone, B Dobson, E Dowler and M Nelson, *Food Projects and How They Work*, York Publishing for Joseph Rowntree Foundation, 1999, p32
43 P McGlone, B Dobson, E Dowler and M Nelson, *Food Projects and How They Work*, York Publishing for Joseph Rowntree Foundation, 1999.
44 V Johnson and J Webster, *'Reaching the parts…' Community Mapping: Working together to tackle social exclusion and food poverty*, Sustain, 2000.
45 Community development worker quoted in P McGlone, B Dobson, E Dowler and M Nelson, *Food Projects and How They Work*, York Publishing for Joseph Rowntree Foundation, 1999, p30
46 B Rogaly, T Fisher and E Mayo, *Poverty, Social Exclusion and Microfinance in Britain*, Oxfam in association with the New Economics Foundation, 1999
47 A Marr, 'The poor and their money: what have we learned?' *ODI Poverty Briefing* no 4, March 1999, Overseas Development Institute, London email publications@odi.org.uk or www.odi.org.uk.
48 H Cooper, S Arber, L Fee and J Ginn, *The Influence of Social Support and Social Capital on Health*, Health Education Authority, 1999; H Joshi, R D Wiggins, M Bartley, R Mitchell, S Gleve and K Lynch, 'Putting health inequalities on the map: does where you live matter, and why?' in: H Graham (ed), *Understanding Health Inequalities*, Open University Press, 2001
49 Consultation document obtainable from Department of Health, PO Box 777, London SE1 6XH or from www.doh.gov.uk
50 Scientific Advisory Committee on Nutrition, Department of Health, 2001, *Government Initiatives in Nutrition*, tabled for meeting 12/13 June 2001, p30
51 J McLeish, *Report of the Welfare Foods Consultative Conference*, Maternity Alliance, 2000
52 Maternity Alliance, *Women and Children First: Briefing paper on health inequalities among mother and babies in the UK*, Maternity Alliance, 2000
53 See note 4
54 See note 3
55 C Hertzman, 'The case for an early childhood development strategy', ISUMA, *Canadian Journal of Policy Research*, 1, 2, pp11-18; D Ross, P Roberts and K Scott, 2000, 'Family income and child well-being', ISUMA, *Canadian Journal of Policy Research*, 1, 2, pp51-54
56 J Blythman, 'Hello goodness, goodbye grease', *The Sunday Herald*, 13 February 2000, quoted in J McCormick (ed), *Healthy Food Policy: on Scotland's Menu?*, Scottish Council Foundation with the Joseph Rowntree Foundation, 2000, p51
57 Lone mother in letter to CPAG, quoted in W McMahon and T Marsh, *Filling the Gap: Free school meals, nutrition and poverty*, CPAG, 1999, p13

58 J McCormick (ed), *Healthy Food Policy: on Scotland's menu?*, Scottish Council Foundation with the Joseph Rowntree Foundation, 2000

59 Consultation material is available on the Food Standards Agency website: www.foodstandards.gov.uk

60 Food Commission, 'Checkout: parents beware!', 3 page special in *Food Magazine*, 53, April/June 2001, pp11-13; J McCormick in: J McCormick (ed), *Healthy Food Policy: On Scotland's menu?*, Scottish Council Foundation with the Joseph Rowntree Foundation, 2000 pp 49-56

61 G Tansey and T Worsley, *The Food System*, Earthscan, 1995

62 J McCormick (ed), *Healthy Food Policy: On Scotland's menu?*, Scottish Council Foundation with the Joseph Rowntree Foundation, 2000, p51

63 Sustain, *TV Dinners: What's being served up by the advertisers?*, Sustain, 2001

64 P Storey and R Chamberlin, *Improving the Take Up of Free School Meals*, Research Report 270, DfEE, 2001

65 W McMahon and T Marsh, *Filling the Gap: Free school meals, nutrition and poverty*, CPAG, 1999

66 CPAG, *Free School Meals in Scotland Briefing*, February 2000 (available at www.cpag.org.uk)

67 See note 64

68 Joe Harvey, director of Health Education Trust, personal communication, March 2001

69 See note 64

70 C Street and P Kenway, *Food for Thought – Breakfast Clubs And Their Challenges*, New Policy Institute, 1999

71 See note 70

72 See note 70

73 S A Turner, R Levinson, B McLellan Arnold, S Stevenson, A Donkin and E Dowler, 'Healthy eating in primary schools', *Health Education Journal*, September, 2000, 59, 3, pp1-15

74 See note 73

75 See note 73

76 Caroline Walker Trust, Eating well for looked after children and young people: nutritional and practical guidelines, 2001. CWT, PO BOX 61, St Austell, PL26 6YL or www.cwt.org.uk

77 Scottish Community Diet Project, *Breakfast Clubs...a Head Start*, SCDP, 2001 available from tel: 0141 226 5261, email scdp@scotconsumer. org.uk or website www.dietproject.co.uk; National Food Alliance (now Sustain), *Making Links: A toolkit for local food projects*, Sustain, 1999

78 For example, J Moe, J Roberts and L Moore, 'Planning and running fruit tuck shops in primary schools', *Health Education*, 101, 2, 2001, pp61-68

79 J Boyd Orr, *Food Health and Income*, Macmillan and Co. Ltd, 1936, pp49 and 50; E Dowler and S Leather, 'Spare some change for a bite to eat? From Primary Poverty to Social Exclusion: the role of food', in J Bradshaw and R Sainsbury (eds), *Experiencing Poverty*, Ashgate, 2000, pp 200-218